Leckie×Leckie
Scotland's leading educational publishers

Success guides

Standard Grade
# Craft & Design

David McMillan ✕ Mark Leishman

# Contents

# Contents

## Chapter 5: Hand Tools

## Index

# Introduction

## Standard Grade Craft & Design course outline

Standard Grade Craft & Design is a subject that will offer you the opportunity to solve practical problems through designing and making products. It will help you to be more aware of the contribution and influence that design and technology has on your own life and on society. Throughout the course you should be given the opportunity to think creatively and to be inventive. You should be encouraged to design and make products which are unique and clearly your own. Creating a product which is original and useful is a demanding task and will require that you have some knowledge of how to design and communicate ideas effectively. You will also need to be knowledgeable about tools, machines, materials and manufacturing processes and be able to demonstrate the skills necessary to make the product yourself.

The course is divided into three parts.

* Practical skills
* Designing
* Knowledge and understanding

Each of these three parts will be assessed and graded separately before you will be awarded an overall grade by the Scottish Qualifications Authority (SQA) at the end of your course. You will be required to design and make several products during your course. The design folios that you produce will be assessed by your teacher against a national standard and the grades that you get may be checked by the SQA before you are awarded a final grade for the Designing component of the course. Your craft work will be assessed in a similar way and this will lead to a final grade being awarded for Practical Abilities. There is no external examination for either of these two components. Your ability to design and manufacture products will be assessed through your course work.

There is, however, a written final examination to test your knowledge and understanding of these two components of the course. You will sit this examination in the May or June after you finish the course. Standard Grade Craft & Design is examined at three different levels – Foundation, General and Credit. Usually candidates will be presented at two levels, either Foundation/General or General/Credit. Each of the three papers will last one hour.

It is important that you revise and study for these examinations and this book has been written to help you with this. This is a revision guide and is presented in a format that is easy to read and find information from. The notes are short and concise and in many cases presented in list format to make it easy for you to remember the main facts. You will have your own notes from class, you will have watched many demonstrations and have observed other people in your class carry out tasks and activities that were different from your own. Also, you will have, of course, your own experiences from the work that you have undertaken in class and at home, but you should remember that you will not have experienced everything in the course and you will have to learn some things from a class demonstration or from a book.

Exam-style questions have been placed throughout the book to help you test your understanding as you go.

# Design, step by step

*'All that we do almost all of the time is design, for design is basic to all human activity.'*  **Victor Papanek**

That statement is so true when we begin to think about our lives. We all get up in the morning and make decisions about what to wear according to what we are going to do and where we are going that day. We often accessorise to reflect our personality and lifestyle. We live in houses where the things in it have been chosen to fit with the space and layout of each room. We live in neighbourhoods where gardens have been styled with flowers and the hedges and lawns cut into interesting shapes and patterns. Even simple decisions about where to hang a picture in a room and how best to decorate a cake all show that design is something that plays an important part in our lives.

## The role of the designer

We all make simple design decisions every day without ever stopping to consider the process we go through in our minds before making those decisions. Designers are people who make decisions to solve real problems but have to do it in a structured way so that the products they design meet the needs of other people. This means that they must carefully analyse what is to be done, research information, discuss their ideas with others, test their proposals and evaluate their solutions. This is perhaps a simplistic way of looking at what a designer does and we must realise that within each of these activities there will be lots for the designer to do.

## Main stages

The diagram below sets out the main stages in the design process. This may reflect your own experiences as you designed and made your own products.

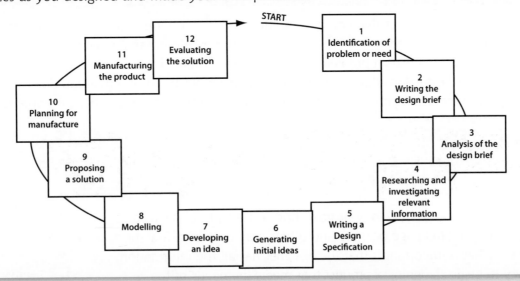

## Quick Test

1. Apart from at the end, where else in the design process might you evaluate your design?

2. Apart from sketching, give two other ways that a designer would communicate the proposed solution to a client.

# The design brief

## The starting point

A design brief can be thought of as a statement which tells the designer **what** is to be designed, **who** it is to be designed for and **where** it is to be used. It need not contain a lot of information and can be left very **open**, allowing the designer scope to be creative and original. The design brief is often thought of as the starting point of the design process. It can be something that is written by the designer or something that is given to the designer by a **client**.

## Problem solving

Very often a design brief is written as a result of someone having identified a **problem** that needs to be solved or a **need** that will improve a situation. It can also be written by a company which has identified an opportunity in the market place to sell a new product. This may be as straightforward as designing a product that is fashionable at the time and is in demand. This is often referred to as a **want** product.

During your course you may have been given a design brief by your teacher and you may also have experienced writing your own brief in response to a task or project that you have been set. Both of these approaches are very useful and reflect what happens in industry. Designers can be given design briefs by the people they work for and as a result may have to design products that they themselves neither need nor want. They may also be given the freedom to do their own thing by identifying a need, want or market opportunity and designing a product that meets this.

## Be practical and useful

Always discuss a design brief that you have written with other people. Just because you think that it is a good idea doesn't mean that it is. Be clear in your own mind that what you are proposing to do meets a need, answers a problem and has market potential. You need to be aware of any requirements and restrictions that your product may have but be careful that you don't include unnecessary restrictions in your brief that may prevent you from being creative and original.

## Make sure you have the information you need

There are no rules as to how long or how short a design brief needs to be. Some can run to a full page or more and others may only be a few short sentences. What is important is that the designer has all the information necessary to begin designing a product that meets the needs of the customer or client.

**Top Tip**
The design brief should give information about **what** the design is for, **who** will use it and **where** it might be used.

## Quick Test

1. What is the purpose of the design brief?
2. Give two pieces of information that might be contained in a design brief.

**Answers: 1.** This is a short statement that tells the designer what is to be designed. **2.** (i) Who the product is intended for. (ii) Where the product is to be used.

# Research

## Important information

Once you have analysed the design brief and are clear about the type of product you are going to design, you need to gather all the information necessary to make your product a success. It is very unlikely that you would design a product that required no research work or additional knowledge. There are lots of different ways that you can collect information and you will need to plan how you are going to go about this task. There are two main ways that you can carry out research: **desk research** and **field research**. Each involves different types of activities and different ways of working.

## Desk research

As the name suggests, this type of work can be carried out at a desk. It usually means that you can gather information without any input or advice from anyone else. This may involve collecting information from the internet, books and journals or recording data found in manuals or from surveys. You will usually be collecting information that has already been recorded by someone else.

## Field research

Here you will need to be more active. You may have to go out and conduct your own survey or ask people their opinion about something. You may need to measure a product or a space and record the result. You may also test something or carry out an evaluation of an existing product and write your own report on it. In some cases you are finding out the information for the first time.

## Using your research

Be careful not to collect information that you are not going to use. This is a common mistake. Only record information that you are going to use. Be selective with what you include in your folio. You will be given credit for including information that is relevant. It will be recognised that, in order to include only relevant information, you will have excluded many other things. If you include everything that you find on a topic and only a small percentage of it is relevant to your design work, it may not be obvious to whoever is reading your work that you know what is important.

### Analyse, establish, decide

- Carefully analyse your design brief and decide what information you need to find out.
- Establish what information can be obtained from desk research and field research.
- If you are going to carry out a survey, decide what questions to ask those who take part.

## Quick Test

1. Write down two pieces of information that a designer would need to find out before designing a bathroom cabinet.

2. Scale ergonomes are sometimes used to find information about the sizes and proportions of the human body. Write down two other ways of finding such information.

**Answers: 1.** (i) how much space is available on the wall in the bathroom where the cabinet is to be used. (ii) the size of the cabinet is where the bathroom where the things that are likely to be stored in the cabinet. **2.** (i) look up anthropometric data in books and charts (ii) measure a range of people.

# Critical sizes

## Areas of investigation

During research work you will discover that sizes and measurements play an important part in determining whether or not your final design will be successful. There is a lot to consider and you should approach this part of your research work logically and be sure that you have all of the critical sizes needed to allow your design to function well and do the job that it is intended for.

Even the most simple product will require you to establish critical sizes and you should consider five areas for investigation before you begin your design work.

## 1. Location

Find out as much as you can about where your design is likely to be used. Of course designers have no control over how or where a product will be used once it has been sold, but they can anticipate the size restrictions that may exist in the most likely place that the product will be used. For example, if you were to design a bathroom cabinet for use in a family home it would be impossible to design one that fits perfectly into every bathroom. However, by establishing what type of family home it is intended for, you will be able to focus on that type of household and find out what maximum size of cabinet would fit in that particular kind of bathroom.

## 2. Ergonomics

This area of research is more important for some products than others but it must be considered for every product where there is likely to be interaction with people. Clearly there is less human interaction with a bathroom cabinet than there would be with a dining room chair for example. Nevertheless any critical sizes that are required need to be clearly established. For example, considering a person's maximum reach and height will help you to establish the position of door handles, the size and position of a mirror and the height of the top shelf of a cabinet. You will also find it useful to look at anthropometric data especially when considering the 5th and 95th percentile person.

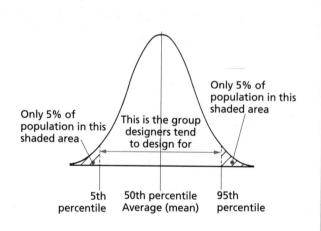

Only 5% of population in this shaded area

This is the group designers tend to design for

Only 5% of population in this shaded area

5th percentile

50th percentile Average (mean)

95th percentile

## 3. Interaction with other products

As well as interacting with people, products also have to come into contact with and interact with other products. A bathroom cabinet will probably have to store deodorant bottles, bars of soap toothpaste and other similar items of toiletries. Therefore it is important that the designer knows what these products are and measures them. This will help to establish the minimum size and distance between shelves.

# 4. Existing products that do the same job

There is always the risk that you design a new product that does not perform as well as similar products already in the market place. New products need to be tested and evaluated in a number of ways to find out if they do their job well and perform as expected. This can take time and cause a lot of unnecessary trial and error for the designer. Much can be learned from existing products, and measuring them to establish key sizes can be useful. You will find it very useful to test and evaluate a range of existing bathroom cabinets to find out what is already available in the market place. In doing this you can measure and record useful dimensions such as cabinet height, shelf width and the distance between the shelves. This does not mean that you have to use these sizes, but it will provide you with useful information with which you can make your own decisions.

# 5. Standard components

Most products use standard components that have been mass produced as part of their design. Items such as screws, door handles, mirrors, brackets and light bulb holders are all products that already exist and can be bought and used as part of your design. It is possible to redesign these standard items and customise them but this is expensive and time consuming. Standard components that might be used in a bathroom cabinet include the plastic runners for doors, door hinges, handles, mirrors, screws and knockdown fittings. There may be more standard components but you must establish which you are going to use and find out their size before you begin your design work.

**Top Tip**

Build around the critical sizes that are important to your design. You may find it useful to do a full size drawing first, even if this means sticking several sheets of paper together.

# Establishing critical sizes

- Measure a space in a similar location to establish a maximum area available for your product.
- You can pretend to use your new product. This will help you to get an idea of maximum and minimum sizes that will make it easy for people to use.
- Measure products that are likely to be held, stored, displayed or to come in contact with your new design.
- Find a similar product that does its job well and measure what sizes have been used.
- Don't forget to design around your standard components. Know their sizes.

## Quick Test

1. Give two important dimensions that will need to be found when designing a chair to be used in a school dining room.

**Answers: 1.** (i) The height of the dining table (ii) the popliteal height of the 5th and 95th percentile person who is likely to sit in the chair.

# Aesthetics

## Understanding aesthetics

Aesthetics is the word used when explaining or thinking about the appearance of an object. Nature creates objects with beautiful aesthetics with ease, but creating man-made objects with good aesthetics can be more problematic.

A good understanding of aesthetics is important when designing. How a design looks creates our first impression and helps us to form opinions about the design. Although aesthetics can be very personal to the individual ('beauty is in the eye of the beholder'), careful research can identify suitable aesthetics for a group of similar individuals or a target market.

Aesthetics is not simply about making a product look eye-catching. The appearance of a product can suggest more about a product than you may think. By using the correct visual elements a designer can make products look fast, strong, light, durable, safe, clean etc. It can be difficult to appreciate how a designer has used aesthetics in this way. However, aesthetics can be broken into elements such as: line, shape and form, size and proportion, symmetry, colour, pattern and texture, and style.

Understanding how we react to different combinations of these elements allows designers to make products appealing.

## Visual elements of aesthetics

### Line

Lines are often used to create and develop design ideas. They can be arranged and combined to create different shapes or textures, convey emotion or suggest movement. Lines are not limited to paper, but also can be seen and appreciated on the products themselves. Products can be said to have clean lines, sharp lines, soft edges, smooth curves etc. Designers can use lines to create illusions of speed, comfort or space, amongst other things.

### Shape and form

Shape and form will have a huge impact on the success of a design project. The consideration of shape is often used as a starting point in design work. Manipulating and experimenting with shape can provide the initial aesthetic of a design project. Shapes are two-dimensional (flat) and can be characterised as:

- geometric: triangles, rectangles, circles, etc.
- natural: leaves, flowers, plants, etc.
- man-made.

Shape can also be developed into different forms. Form is three-dimensional, displaying length, breadth and height. Three-dimensional form is how we view the most of the world around us. Forms can be categorized as:

- geometric: pyramids, cuboids, spheres, etc.
- natural: shells, leaves, flowers, plants, etc.
- man-made or stylised forms.

Form does more than help create the look of a product. It will impact and influence many issues such as function, ease of use, manufacture and costs. For example, the aerodynamic form of a car improves its efficiency. Carefully developed soft rounded forms make comfortable edges on handles.

Some designs may look fantastic but would prove to be difficult to make and cost too much.

## Size and proportion

The size of an object is found by measuring its dimensions. Size does not have the same impact on the appearance of an object as proportion. Proportion is the relationship between the length, breadth and height of an object. This is more important to the overall appearance of an object. Proportion is so important that throughout history scientific and mathematical theories have been developed to create perfect proportions. The Greeks created the **golden section** which was used in their architecture and the Italian Renaissance provided the **Fibonacci number sequence**, used in art and architecture to express perfect proportions.

## Symmetry and balance

Symmetry and balance are important; our brains are critical of designs that do not appear to visually balance. Symmetrical designs are identical on each side (they are a mirror image of each other). This is the simplest way to ensure a visual balance. However, symmetrical objects can appear less exciting as the brain does not have to work very hard to understand them. Asymmetrical designs are more interesting to look at but require some expertise from the designer to make us accept them.

Balance does not need to be confined to a balance created between left and right. Many natural forms display radial balance growing from a central point to create circular or spiral-type patterns.

## Colour

Colour can have a huge impact on a design and needs to be considered carefully. It has the potential to improve or spoil a design.

The choice of colour can be influenced by previous associations, e.g. red is hot, blue is cold, green is healthy, orange is warm. Colour can also be chosen for effect, e.g. red is advancing, blue is receding, green is relaxing, yellow is stimulating.

The colour spectrum can be divided into primary, secondary and tertiary colours. Primary colours are the colours that, when mixed, make all other colours. The three primary colours are red, blue and yellow – no colours can be mixed to make these colours. By mixing the primary colours you create the secondary colours, which are violet, green and orange. Mixing the primary and secondary colours creates the tertiary colours.

The colour spectrum can be displayed on a colour wheel which can be used to choose suitable colour combinations. Colours can harmonise, contrast or complement each other, depending on the desired effect. Harmonising colours are close together on the colour wheel, while the further apart colours are, the greater the contrast; directly opposite colours are complimentary.

Adding white to a colour creates a tint and adding black creates a tone.

## Pattern and texture

Pattern can be used to create interest, and liven up plain areas of a design. Pattern can also be applied to improve the function or durability of a design – patterned surfaces may be less likely to show dirt or stains. Patterns can be created randomly or deliberately using geometry and repetition. Like pattern, texture can be used for more than creating an interesting surface. Adding texture to handles can provide better grip, while applying texture to plastics can make them appear to be more like expensive natural materials.

## Style

A style is created by all the visual elements that contribute to aesthetics. A style is a look popular for a period of time, usually linked to fashion. Popular styles of the past include Art Nouveau, Art Deco, Bauhaus, and Modernism. Individual designers can also develop styles of their own which make them popular.

Knowledge and understanding about the effects of colour, texture and form can make a huge difference to your design project.

Tiffany lamp inspired by natural shape and form.

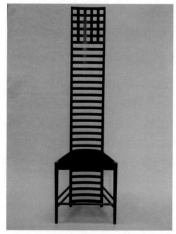

Macintosh uses elegant proportions and positive and negative space to good effect in his ladder-back chair.

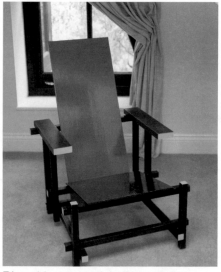

Rietveld uses straight lines and geometric shapes in his red/blue chair.

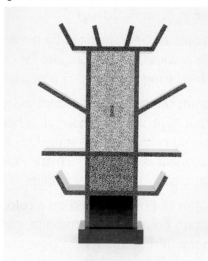

Patterns and bright colours are used in this Memphis unit.

## Quick Test

1. Explain why a designer might use contrast in his design work.

2. Give two examples of contrast and of how it has been used to improve an object.

3. From your own studies, identify three objects that have been created using:
   (i) organic curvilinear shape and forms;
   (ii) geometric shape and form.

**Answers: 1.** To attract attention to a product. **2.** Start and stop buttons (in contrasting colours), smooth and rough textures showing where an object should be held. **3.** See your own course notes.

# Ergonomics

## People and their surroundings

Ergonomics is the study of how people use and interact with objects in their surroundings. The application and understanding of ergonomics has created designs which are easier to use, safer and more efficient.

When considering ergonomics, it is important to identify the most important interactions that will affect the use of the design project. Each design project will require a different set of interactions. The interactions required to use an alarm clock are very different from those of a school desk or chair. Careful study through observation and trials will identify what is important and what is not.

Humans interact with objects and their surroundings using their senses. There are five senses; each gives a different type of feedback about the design:

- sight
- touch
- hearing
- taste
- smell

Sight and touch are often considered to be the most important senses to consider when developing a design proposal. Sight is obviously required to evaluate the aesthetics and to determine how to use and interact with a design project. Touch is necessary to provide feedback and reassurance about interactions. It is also used to determine the finish and quality of a design project.

Sight and touch are considered to be the most important senses when designing but the other three can be just as important.

To make sure the user will be able to interact with the design comfortably without strain or injury, the designer will have consider the user's physical size, weight, range of movements and strength.

## Anthropometrics

Anthropometrics is the study of human sizes, proportion and range of movements. Information about men, women and children of all ages has been gathered and presented in the form of tables of anthropometric data.

Through knowledge and understanding a designer can select the dimensions and data that is appropriate to his or her design work. Selecting the correct data will allow people of all shapes and sizes to interact with a design comfortably and safely. Some of the most commonly used data when beginning a design project are: height, eye level, elbow height, popliteal (back of the knee) height, reach, hand size etc.

The aim of the designer is to ensure that as many people as possible can use the design without discomfort. This is done by considering the range of users, the interactions and selecting the correct percentile ranges. The use of percentile ranges allows the design to be used by up to 95% of the population.

There is no point designing for Mr or Mrs average – they don't exist. A person of average height will not necessarily be average weight or have the average shoe size. Basing a design's dimensions on average sizes would only make it suitable for 50% of the population.

# The 5th to 95th percentile

This refers to the use of a normal distribution curve in determining the correct sizes for a design. This normal distribution curve can be applied to any physical dimension of the human body. Depending on the purpose of the design, the designer will choose either the 5th, 50th or 95th percentile range. The 5% at each end of the scale are not considered important as there are only a limited number of people with these dimensions.

## Using anthropometric data

When designing a doorway the designer would have to consider:

- what interactions are required?
- what would cause discomfort?
- what would be the most suitable percentile range?

5%          95%

0  10  20  30  40  50  60  70  80  90 100%

| Body Feature | Male, Percentile | | |
|---|---|---|---|
| | 5th | 50th | 95th |
| A Stature | 1625 | 1740 | 1855 |
| B Sitting height | 850 | 910 | 970 |
| C Knee height, sitting | 495 | 540 | 590 |
| D Popliteal height | 400 | 440 | 480 |
| E Elbow rest height | 190 | 240 | 285 |
| F Thigh clearance | 125 | 150 | 175 |
| G Buttock-knee length | 540 | 595 | 645 |
| H Buttock-popliteal length | 440 | 495 | 550 |
| I Forearm to forearm | 390 | 450 | 510 |
| J Hip breadth | 315 | 360 | 400 |
| K Weight (lbs) | 145 | 181 | 217 |

(all sizes in millimetres)

Select the required sizes from the relevant tables.

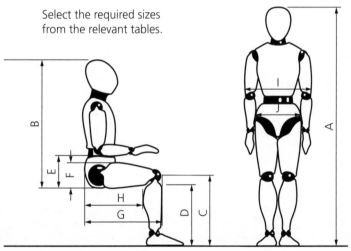

Seated figure for chair design       Standing figure used for doorway

Walking forwards through the door without the need to stoop is the desired outcome. So the 95th percentile male height and shoulder width would ensure that most people would get through the door comfortably – only a very few would have to stoop.

If the designer was determining the height of a shelf, he or she would not base it in the 95th percentile male height, as this would put it out of reach for all but the tallest people. He or she would base it on the reach of the 5th percentile woman.

Most designs are not based on one single percentile range, as most require a combination of the 5th and 95th percentiles to ensure their comfortable use. Seating is a good example of this.

A seat will need to:

- support the weight of the person sitting on it – based on the weight of the 95th percentile male;
- allow feet to touch the ground – based on the popliteal height of the 5th percentile woman;

- have clearance between the seat and the back of the knee – based on the buttock-to-knee length of the 5th percentile woman;
- be wide enough to sit on – based on the hip breadth of the 95th percentile woman;
- provide lumbar support– based on a compromise between the 5th and 95th percentile.

The 50th percentile is rarely used as it excludes a large percentage of the population. However, it is used for some hand-held objects and handles that require good grip, such as tool handles, handle bars, kettle handles, etc.

Applying ergonomics and anthropometrics should be considered during the development stages of your design through the use of ergonomes and scale models. However, greater focus on anthropometrics will be towards the end of the design process when anthropometric data are likely to be used to develop full-scale working drawings. Evaluation of ergonomics can only be achieved through observing human interaction with full-scale models or prototypes.

The 50th percentile should be used when designing a hand drill.

## Top Tip

Identify important human interactions early in the design process. Using similar or existing products will help highlight key interaction and percentile ranges essential to the success of your project.

## Quick Test

1. Ergonomics will be considered during the development of a new mobile phone.

   (a) Explain why it would be important to consider ergonomics in the design of a new phone.

   (b) List three human interactions which would be considered when developing a design for a new mobile phone.

   (c) Describe what anthropometric data would be required to determine the size and position of the new phone's buttons.

2. Percentile ranges are often used by designers to determine appropriate sizes for their designs.

   (a) At what stage of the design process would percentile ranges most likely be used?

   (b) If the height and width of a classroom door were based on the 50th percentile, would it be suitable for 5%, 50% or 95% of the population?

**Answers: 1. (a)** To makes sure it would fit comfortably in users' hand and be easy to use. **(b)** Sight; to see the screen and position of buttons. Hearing; to ensure that the sound of the phone is clear to the user. Touch; to give feedback about physical interactions. **(c)** The range of movements of users' fingers to make interaction with buttons and controls comfortable. Size and length of fingers to determine size and position of buttons.
**2. (a)** During the development of the full-scale drawing of working prototype. **(b)** Around 50% of the population.

# The design specification

## Do, be and have

Writing the design specification is an important stage in the design process. It can be seen as the link between all of your research work and the creative work that leads to a proposed solution and ultimately a final product. A specification should clearly state what a product must **do**, what it must **be** and what it must **have**. It also provides an opportunity for the designer to outline some personal preferences and wishes for the product. All of these things can be discussed with the client, manufacturer, retailer and other members of the design team. The specification can be viewed as a list of rules that all of the people who have an interest and involvement in a product's design can agree on and then begin to work towards.

## Use a list

A specification should be referred to throughout the design process and used as an evaluation tool once the proposed solution has been finalised. At Standard Grade a specification is usually written in list form and consists of simple short sentences which state clearly the requirements of the product. It is important to be as accurate and as clear as possible, avoiding any statements that are confusing and not **specific** enough. For example, in the design of a desk clock, how useful is it to write the following into the specification?

*The desk clock must be stable.*

How stable should the desk clock really be? Although no specific value can be given here, it would be useful to give something that the reader has experience of and can relate to.

*The desk clock should be stable enough to withstand normal everyday knocks and bumps to the desk.*

This is a much clearer and more specific statement and can easily be used to evaluate the success of any final product. It is important that you give as much information as you can when you write a specification. Each point that you make should offer some criteria (where possible) to measure or test if the final product meets these requirements.

### Be thorough

Write your specification based on information that you have found during your research work. Don't guess things. Be thorough in your work. Be careful not to leave out anything and try wherever possible to give some criteria around which your final idea can be evaluated and checked.

**Top Tip**
Your specification can be a very useful evaluation tool. Check and test your finished design against all the points in your specification.

## Quick Test

**1.** Write down two points that should be included in the design specification for a baby's highchair.

**Answers: 1.** (i) The chair must be stable enough not fall over easily when knocked or rocked by the baby. (ii) The highchair must be easily cleaned and should not have any dirt traps.

# Initial ideas

## Stimulating ideas

Many people find putting their first ideas down on paper very difficult and struggle to be original and creative. It is not always easy to resist the temptation to sketch ideas which are familiar and perhaps already exist. Lots of new and familiar ideas can go through your head very quickly and some of these can get lost before you have had the time get them down on paper. Often you will need to use very quick sketching methods, and sacrifice quality for quantity and speed in order to record all of your ideas. You may find that generating new ideas from your imagination becomes difficult and that you require some other kind of stimulus to help you.

## Inspiration

The following example shows a Standard Grade pupil using influences from the natural world to help design a chair. On the following pages are picture boards of a variety of interesting shapes and forms taken from an internet image search. You are able to see on the pages that follow how some of these images have stimulated this pupil's imagination to come up with initial ideas for a chair. This pupil has gone to the trouble of sticking down photos from the image board beside the sketches. This clearly shows where the ideas came from. Notice how quick and simple some of the sketches are. There is no need at this stage to spend time on presentation-style drawings and sketches.

**Top Tip**
Don't be afraid to make mistakes with your initial ideas. Be creative and get things down on paper quickly. This is your chance to experiment and try things out.

## Image boards collected by a Standard Grade pupil

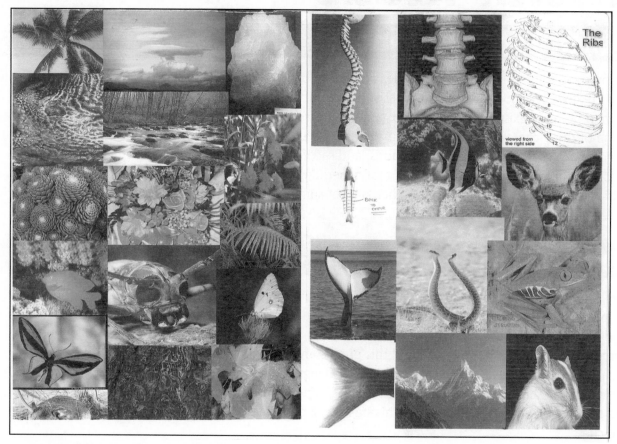

## Initial ideas created from image board

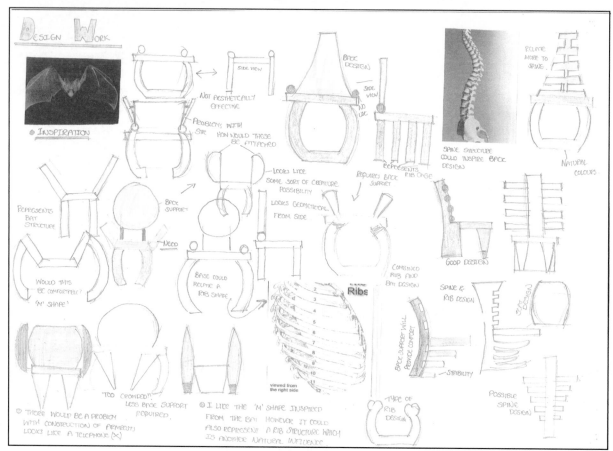

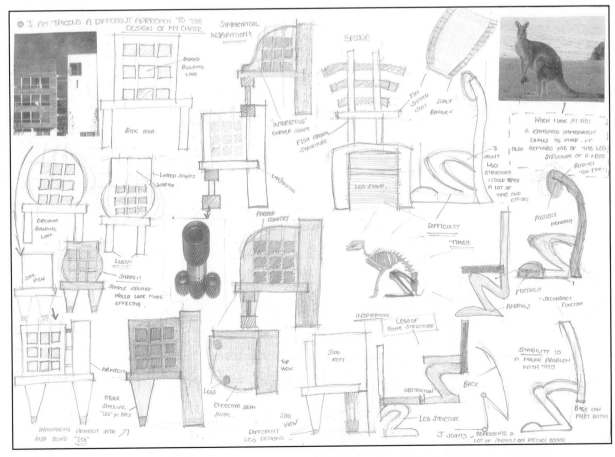

# Developing ideas

## Experimenting with ideas

After discussing your initial ideas with a variety of people you will begin to see one or two ideas emerging that have the potential to work. It is important that you take time to experiment further with these ideas and begin the evolutionary process of developing your ideas into a solution that meets the requirements of the design brief. Don't accept that your first idea is your best.

## Record your decisions

There is a lot to consider during this development stage, and you will need to keep referring back to your specification to check if your ideas and the changes you make to them meet the requirements. You should comment on decisions you make on areas such as **function**, **aesthetics**, **manufacturing**, **construction** and **complexity**. Indeed, any decision that you make or opinion that you have on anything to do with the development of your design should be recorded at this stage.

Notice that throughout the development of the chair design this pupil is continually writing down his thoughts and decisions about everything as they occur.

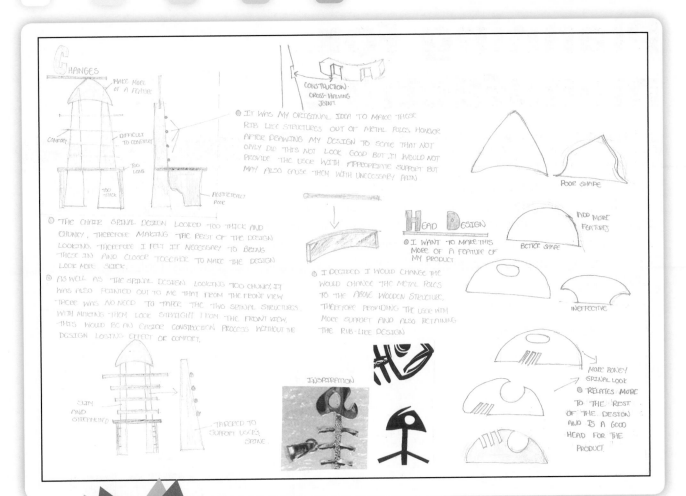

**Top Tip**
Write down all your questions, thoughts and decisions on things like construction, materials, aesthetics, ergonomics, function and manufacturing. You will attract marks for the things you say as well as the things you sketch and draw.

# Planning for manufacture

## Equipment and resources

This is the stage in the design process when you will need to consult with your teacher to discuss the idea that you have, and ensure that it is suitable for manufacture with the equipment and resources that you have at your disposal. You will then need to produce a scale orthographic drawing of your design and a cutting list. It is also useful at this stage to produce at least an outline sequence of operations explaining how you propose to make your design and what materials, tools and processes will be used.

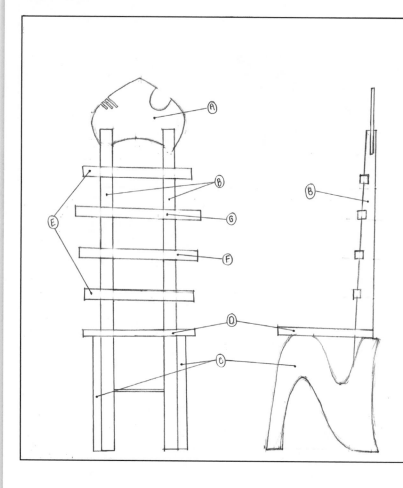

| PART | No. OFF | MATERIAL | DIMENSIONS (mm) |
|------|---------|----------|-----------------|
| A | 1 | HARDWOOD | 360 × 230 × 10 |
| B | 2 | HARDWOOD | 1075 × 80 × 35 |
| C | 2 | HARDWOOD | 427 × 400 × 21 |
| D | 1 | HARDWOOD | 380 × 415 × 22 |
| E | 2 | HARDWOOD | 400 × 40 × 45 |
| F | 1 | HARDWOOD | 415 × 40 × 45 |
| G | 1 | HARDWOOD | 430 × 40 × 45 |
| H | 1 | DOWEL | 190 × Ø 22 |

**Top Tip**
Cutting lists should give information about the material, size and numbers required of each part.

## Sequence Of Operations

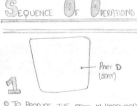

**1**

Part D (Seat)

- To produce the seat in hardwood, you:
  - Acquire pieces of oak that can be used and glue them together to make a piece of material large enough to make the seat
  - Plane the glued oak using a planer.
  - Create a template of the shape of the seat and use this to mark out the shape onto the oak.
  - Cut out shape using a band saw
  - Plane edges and surface using a smoothing plane for the edges and a jack plane for the surface
  - Smooth down front and back of the seat, firstly using rough sand paper and then fine-grain sand paper.

**2**

Part B (Spine back support)

- To produce the spine back support, you:
  - Acquire a piece of hardwood and cut off a piece using the band saw big enough to make the support.
  - Prepare this piece using a planer.
  - Create a template of the shape and mark this on to the oak.
  - Cut out the shape using band saw

- Plane all edges of the back support using a jack plane
- Remove marks using rough sand paper and smooth over surface using fine-grained paper.
- Repeat process to manufacture another spine back support

**3**

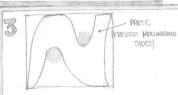

Part C (Freisitz Mollinissimo sides)

- Create a template of shape and use this to mark out shape on to 9mm MDF with a veneer.
- Drill holes using a pillar drill and a forstner drill bit on shaded parts of material shown above.
- Cut out shape using a band saw.
- File edges using half round file and then sand.
- Repeat process to manufacture 2nd Freisitz Mollinissimo

**4**

Parts E, F, G Ribbed back support

- Acquire a large piece of hardwood, big enough to make four ribbed back supports
- Prepare this piece using a planer.
- Create a template for each of the four different ribs.

- Mark the shapes on to the hardwood and cut each one out using a band saw
- Sand the outside edge, using a disc sand and the inside edge, using the edge of the belt sander.
- Finish each piece by hand.

**5**

Joining part D with part B

- Decide on how far from the side of the seat, you want the spine supports to be. Make a mark on the seat, for this position.
- Decide on how far back you wish the seat to go into part B, then using a try square draw a straight line from the mark.
- Measure the width of the spine support at the height you wish the seat to be at and draw a horizontal line, of this distance from the vertical line previously drawn.
- Join up the lines to the back of the seat, by adding a second vertical line.
- Cut up both sides of the marked out notch using a band saw, then remove notch using a bevel edged chisel.
- Repeat on other side to create notch for other spine support

Notch on seat

---

- In order for the back supports to sit flush we also need to take out a notch from the supports.
- Firstly fix the spine supports and seat together and measure the distance from the back of the seat to where the support and seat join.
- Then draw a straight horizontal line from the tapered side of the spinal support using a try square.
- From draw a line from this horizontal line with the same length as the thickness of the chair.
- Remove notches on both spinal supports using the same process as above.

**6**

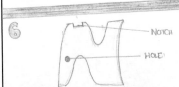

Notch
Hole

- Mark out and drill a hole using a pillar drill on both sides on the location shown above. The holes should be drilled half way through the material, so the depth stop on the pillar drill will need to be set in order to do this
- A dowel of diameter 22mm should then be cut to length using a band saw. The length should the distance between the two sides plus 9mm.
- A notch of depth 7.5mm should then be cut into both sides (above).
- A piece of pine with thickness 15mm and length equalling the distance between the two sides plus the width of both sides.

- On one end of the pine, measure down 7.5mm and draw a line across the wood with a try square
- Measure a distance the same thickness as the sides and draw this line. Draw a line down to the bottom of the pine, creating a shoulder.
- Remove the shoulder using a band saw and repeat on the other side
- On both shoulders drill a hole with the same diameter as a screw.
- On the reverse side drill two holes of the same diameter on the long side of the pine. The holes should be spread apart.
- Drill pilot holes into the seat and both notches on each "side". The pilot holes should meet with their corresponding screw holes.
- Join the whole base structure together.

**7**

Joining ribbed and spinal supports

- Join the base structure to the spinal back supports.
- Rest the ribbed supports onto the two spinal structures in the correct position.

- Obtain a small piece of scrap MDF and use this to mark out the eight notches (two on each) that need to be taken out of the ribs.
- Use a band saw to remove these or use a band saw to cut up both sides of the notch and remove with a bevel edged chisel.

Notches

- Place each notch into the correct notch on the spinal supports and mark out where each rib is to be fixed on to.
- In each of these eight spaces remove thin notches using a band saw.

**8**

- Glue and screw the whole chair structure together
- Apply a few coats of varnish to the whole chair as a finish.

# Evaluation

## Consumer evaluation

Evaluation is something that should be undertaken throughout the design of a product. It would be wrong to leave the evaluation to the end. However, once the product has been made it can be tested and evaluated fully under the conditions in which it is expected to be used. This type of **consumer** or **user evaluation** can be done using the following questions.

- Is the product easy to use?
- Does the product do the job that it is intended to do?
- Is the product safe to use?
- Is the product easy to maintain?
- Is the product attractive?

## Evaluate using the specifications

It is also useful for the designer to evaluate the finished product against the specification. This is important to check that the product does what the design brief has asked it to do and that it meets the needs of the client. It would be normal in this situation to take each specification point in turn and either **test**, **check** or **measure** how well the product performs against it.

## Evaluate manufacture

The last area of evaluation that could be considered for your product is its manufacture. This is likely to be the first time that your design has been made and therefore during manufacture it is possible that you discovered problems or difficulties in making it. This may have led to a change in the design or a change in the way it was manufactured.

### Record evaluation

All of the results from your evaluations and tests should be recorded and presented in a logical way. This information is useful and will provide evidence that your design is suitable and ready to enter the market place.

Evaluation is an important and necessary part of the design process. Even well established products can be improved and updated.

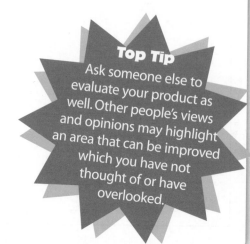

**Top Tip**
Ask someone else to evaluate your product as well. Other people's views and opinions may highlight an area that can be improved which you have not thought of or have overlooked.

## Early Ideas Evaluation.

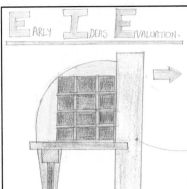

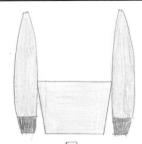

○ THIS DESIGN HAS MAINLY BEEN INFLUENCED BY GEOMETRICAL BUILDINGS OR OBJECTS THAT I HAVE RESEARCHED

○ THE USER SHOULD FEEL COMFORTABLE RESTING AGAINST THE CORNER JOINT

○ STABILITY IS NOT AN ISSUE ESPECIALLY IF THE PART (LABELLED) IS MADE OF A DENSE, HOWEVER THIS COULD MAKE THE CHAIR TIP TO ONE SIDE.

○ THE LARGE ARMREST RESTRICTS MOVEMENT FOR THE USER, AND IT MAY ALSO RESTRICT THE USE OF THE CHAIR TO ONLY CORNERS OF ROOMS.

○ THIS DESIGN WAS INFLUENCED BY A SHAPE THAT OCCURS NATURALLY WHEN A BAT FLAPS ITS WINGS.

○ HOWEVER THIS DESIGN COULD BE THOUGHT OF AS A STOOL, THEREFORE IT DOES NOT MEET MY DESIGN BRIEF.

○ I ALSO MAKE REFERENCE TO A BACK SUPPORT IN MY SPECIFICATION, AND SINCE THIS DESIGN HAS NO BACK SUPPORT THEN IT DOES NOT MEET THIS TARGET.

○ THE BASE OF THIS DESIGN WOULD MOST LIKELY HAVE TO BE MADE FROM CAST ALUMINIUM, WHICH WOULD MAKE A GOOD CONTRAST WITH THE WOODEN SIDES

○ I WILL TAKE THESE POINTS INTO CONSIDERATION WHEN DEVELOPING MY PRODUCT FURTHER.

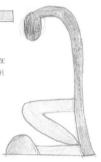

○ THIS DESIGN WAS DERIVED FROM THE BODY SHAPE OF A LEAPING KANGAROO. IT HAS BEEN NATURALLY INFLUENCED.

○ THE BACK SUPPORT OF THIS DESIGN MAY CAUSE PROBLEMS AS IT IS LEANING FORWARD WHICH MAY CAUSE SPINE DAMAGE WHILE IN USE.

○ THE HEAD SUPPORT IS PLACED INCORRECTLY AND IS ACTUALLY SERVING NO PURPOSE. IT WOULD HAVE TO BE REPLACED.

○ THE FOOTREST IS A GOOD IDEA TO INCREASE THE COMFORT FACTOR FOR THE USER. IT MAY BE INCORPORATED INTO LATER DESIGNS.

## Design Proposal

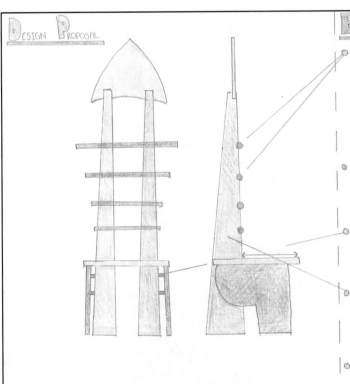

## Evaluation

○ I MADE BACK SUPPORTS OUT OF METAL, INFLUENCED BY RIB STRUCTURES IN MY DESIGN. HOWEVER THESE

  ○ ARE NOT ENTIRELY SAFE SINCE THEY STICK OUT A FAIRLY LARGE DISTANCE, SO COULD BE A HAZARD TO PEOPLE WALKING PAST THE CHAIR

  ○ DO NOT PROVIDE SUFFICIENT BACK SUPPORT AND ARE NOT A SUITABLE MATERIAL FOR THIS PART OF THE DESIGN, SINCE THEY MAY DIG INTO AND CAUSE INJURY OR MAY MARK WALLS IF LEANT AGAINST

○ THE SOLID BASE STRUCTURE MEANS THAT THE DESIGN WILL BE STABLE AND WILL NOT BE KNOCKED OVER EASILY, HOWEVER THE "SIDE" OF THE BASE DOES NOT FIT IN WITH THE REST OF THE DESIGN. THIS IS BECAUSE IT IS GEOMETRICALLY INFLUENCED WHEREAS THE REMAINDER OF THE CHAIR IS NATURALLY INFLUENCED.

○ THE METAL BARS USED IN THE BASE STRUCTURE WILL CONDUCT HEAT ESPECIALLY IF THE CHAIR WAS TO BE USED CLOSE TO A RADIATOR, MEANING THEY WILL BE DANGEROUS TO TOUCH. ALTHOUGH THEY CONTRAST WELL WITH THE WOODEN PARTS OF THE DESIGN, THEY WILL NEED TO BE REPLACED TO PREVENT THIS

○ THE WIDTH OF THE SEAT IS SUFFICIENT ENOUGH TO SUPPORT THE 95th PERCENTILE OF MY MARKET GROUP, HOWEVER I MAY NEED TO ALLOW FOR MORE ROOM FROM THE BACK SUPPORT TO THE FRONT OF THE SEAT, SO THAT THE KNEE JOINTS ARE NOT DAMAGED. SOLVING THIS PROBLEM COULD INCLUDE REDUCING THE THICKNESS OF THE BACK SUPPORT

○ I MAY NEED TO SET THE BACK SUPPORT AT A LARGER ANGLE TO THE SEAT, FOR MORE SUPPORT, HOWEVER NOT TOO FAR BACK, SO THAT THE USER DOES NOT SLIP OFF.

**PRODUCT EVALUATION**

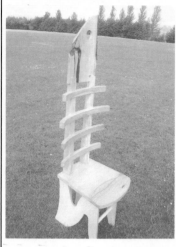

- IS THE PRODUCT EASY TO USE?

- DOES THE PRODUCT LOOK GOOD?
  - THE HARDWOOD USED ON THE CHAIR GIVES IT A NATURAL FEEL AND MAKES IT LOOK IMPRESSIVE

- IS THE PRODUCT EASY TO MAINTAIN?
  - THE VARNISH USED TO FINISH PARTS ON THE PRODUCT MAKES IT EASY TO CLEAN AND TO REMOVE ANY MARKS

- IS IT ERGONOMICALLY WELL DESIGNED?

- IS IT WELL MADE?
  - THE PRODUCT IS WELL FINISHED AND THERE ARE NO LOOSE JOINTS MAKING IT SECURE AND STABLE, MEANING IT IS VERY WELL.

- DOES THE PRODUCT FULFILL ITS FUNCTION?

- THE CHAIR WAS ABLE TO STAND ON ITS OWN BEFORE EACH PART WAS JOINED, THEREFORE WHEN EACH PART IS JOINED IT WILL BE STABLE BOTH IN AND OUT OF USE.

- THE ANGLE OF THE BACK SUPPORT SITS AT AN ANGLE OF BIGGER THAN 90° TO THE USER. THIS STOPS ANY INJURY TO THE USER FROM OCCURING.

- THE SEAT OF THE CHAIR IS AT THE CORRECT HEIGHT ABOVE SO THAT THE USER IS NOT BENDING THEIR KNEES TOO FAR TO CAUSE STRAIN. THIS WAS AN IMPORTANT ERGONOMIC FACTOR THAT I ACHIEVED WELL

- THE CHANGE OF MATERIAL FROM METAL TO OAK WAS A GOOD ONE AS IT COMPLYS WITH MY SPECIFICATION IN BEING A SUITABLE MATERIAL THAT WILL NOT CAUSE STRAIN.

- EACH MATERIAL HAS BEEN USED IN THE CORRECT PLACE, SO NOT TO CONFLICT WITH HAZARDS. MAINLY OAK HAS BEEN USED ON THE PRODUCT SO THIS WILL NOT CONDUCT HEAT AND WILL NOT BE DANGEROUS TO TOUCH

# Presenting solutions

## Presenting and communicating

Taking time to produce a well-presented drawing of any proposed final solution is necessary to communicate the idea clearly to everyone concerned. Designers do this to show their clients what the final idea will look like and use the drawing to discuss any changes or alterations to the design.

There are a variety of ways this can be done but generally the drawings are in full colour and show the product in three dimensions. However, it is also possible to produce a very effective production drawing in two dimensions, like the one shown below.

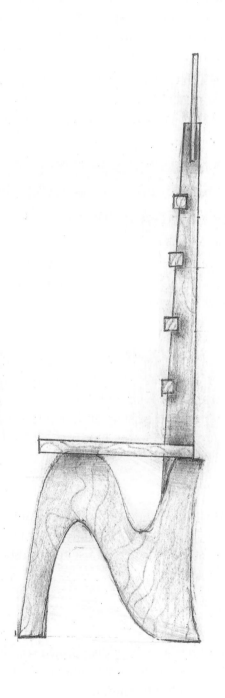

# Wood

Wood has played an important part in the design of products over the years and, despite the development of numerous man-made materials, it remains a very important raw material today.

## Softwoods and hardwoods

Solid timber can be divided into two main groups, softwoods and hardwoods. These names can be misleading, however, as they have nothing to do with the working properties of the timber. For example, balsa wood is a hardwood, but it is soft and dents easily, whilst some softwood timbers are much harder and more robust. Many hardwoods are imported and come from the temperate climates of central Europe and Africa. They are slow-growing, close-grained, timbers making them expensive and very difficult to replace. Most softwood comes from the cooler northern parts of Europe, making them less expensive and more accessible.

Each wood has its own distinctive colour and grain structure. making it a very attractive and desirable material. In selecting the most suitable wood for use in any kind of design work it is essential that its functional and mechanical characteristics are considered carefully.

## Softwoods

### Redwood (Scots Pine)

Its colour varies from a pale yellowy cream to a reddish brown. It has a straight grain and is fairly strong and easy to work with. It is reasonably durable.

### Whitewood (Spruce)

It has a plain creamy colour. Spruce is a very tough material and it is hard and durable. However, it is also prone to twisting and therefore is not particularly suited to outdoor use.

### Douglas Fir

Douglas Fir has a reddish brown appearance. It has a very straight grain and is slightly resinous making it water resistant and therefore suited to use outdoors.

### Red Cedar

This wood has a dark reddish brown colour. It is also a knot-free, straight-grained timber, making it easy to work with. Suited to outdoor use.

# Hardwoods

## Beech

Beech has a pinkish brown colour with flecks of grain through it. It is an extremely hard, tough material which has a close grain. Beech is not easy to work with. Due to its strength, it is particularly suited for use in chairs. Beech is also good for steam bending.

## Oak

A very strong, hard and durable timber which has a light brown colour with a silver grain running through it.

## Ash

Ash has a creamy, light brown appearance. It is a long-grained timber which makes it flexible and tough. Ash is a stable material which makes it suitable for use outdoors.

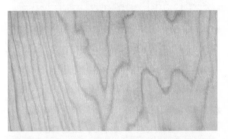

## Teak

This is a durable timber which is very oily. It has a rich, golden brown colour. Teak is hard and strong and very resistant to moisture. Used in high-class furniture.

**Top Tip**

Varnishing wood or sealing the wood in some way will protect it and prevent it from warping and splitting.

## Quick Test

1. Name two conditions that may cause solid wood to warp, change shape or split.

2. Give two properties of solid timber that would have to be considered before selecting it for use on a design.

**Answers: 1.** (i) The wood is exposed to moisture or water. (ii) There is considerable temperature change in the place where the wood is being stored. **2.** (i) How dense and hard the wood is and how able it is to withstand impact. (ii) The wood's colour and how attractive the grain pattern is.

# Metals

## Sources

All metals, except gold, are extracted from chemical compounds containing metal and other elements, known as ores. Often crushing, filtering and heating in a furnace is required to produce pure metals.

- Iron ore (iron oxide) produces iron, which is used to make steel.
- Aluminium ore (bauxite) is used to make aluminium.

## Ferrous and non-ferrous metals

All metals can be split into two categories: **ferrous** and **non-ferrous.**

- Ferrous metals **contain iron** together with other metals or elements. Most ferrous metals are prone to rust and can be identified by using a magnet.
- Non-ferrous metals are metals that **do not contain iron**. They are not magnetic.

The main body of this kettle is stainless steel, with a copper base.

## Pure metals and alloys

Metals can also be categorised as **pure metals** or **alloys.**

- Pure metals contain only one element in the production of the metal. Commonly used pure metals are iron, aluminium, copper, zinc, tin, silver and gold.
- Alloys are metals that contain two or more pure metals or elements. Commonly used alloys are steel, brass, stainless steel and duralumin.

Pure metals do not always have the correct properties required for a design. Adding other metals or elements to a pure metal creates metal alloys which have different properties. Aluminium, for example, is useful as it is light in weight and resistant to corrosion; however, it is not very strong. Adding other elements can create an aluminium alloy that is stronger than steel.

## Properties of metals

- **Hardness** is a measure of how resistant a material is to cutting, wear or indentation.
- **Toughness** is the amount of impact a material can absorb before breaking.
- **Tensile strength** is a measure of how far the metal can be stretched, crushed, twisted or sheared without breaking.
- **Malleability** is a measure of a material's ability to be hammered into shape.
- **Ductility** is a measure of a material's ability to be stretched before breaking.
- **Elasticity** is a measure of how far a material can be stretched and still return to its original length.
- **Conductivity** is a measure of how well a material conducts heat.

A look at some common kitchen objects illustrates how metals play a vital part in our lives.

## Forms of metal

Metals can be bought in a variety of shapes and sizes, e.g. sheets, bars, tubes, rods, strips, angles and sections. There is a wide range of stock sizes, as shaping and altering sizes is difficult and time-consuming. Any design work using metal should be carefully planned around stock material.

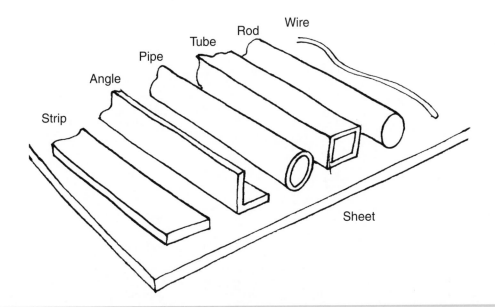

# Properties of pure metals and their uses

| Name | Properties | Uses |
|------|-----------|------|
| Copper | Reddish brown in colour, excellent heat and electrical conductor, malleable and resistant to corrosion after oxidisation (verdigris). | Heating and water pipes, electrical cables, cooking pots and pans, roof coverings. |
| Aluminium | Light grey in colour, lightweight and malleable, a good conductor of heat and electricity. Resistant to corrosion after oxidisation. | Drinks cans, food containers, aluminium foil, car engine parts, aircraft construction, window frames, bike frames and components. |
| Tin | Whitish in colour, soft, resistant to corrosion, non-toxic. | Coating on sheet steel to prevent rust. |
| Lead | Dark grey in colour, heavy, resistant to corrosion, malleable and easy to work into shape when cold. | Weights, roof coverings and flashing. |
| Zinc | Bluish white in colour, resistant to corrosion after oxidation, ductile. | Coating for galvanised steel to prevent rust. |

**Top Tip**
Some metals are easier to work with than others. When selecting a metal for your project consider carefully how it will be shaped and formed as well as its other properties.

# Alloys: their composition, properties and uses

| Name | Composition | Properties | Uses |
|------|-------------|------------|------|
| Mild steel | Iron containing up to 0.3% carbon. | Easy to work, malleable, tough with high tensile strength. | Construction, nuts and bolts and drop forging. |
| High carbon steel | Iron containing from 0.7% to 1.4% carbon. | Hard but less malleable, can be heat-treated to increase hardness and toughness. | Hammers, chisels, drills and files. |
| Stainless steel | Iron containing chromium and nickel. | Hard, tough and resistant to corrosion. | Kitchen sinks, fixtures and fittings and worktops. |
| Brass | Copper containing 35% zinc. | Yellow in colour, resistant to corrosion, good electrical conductor, hard, easy to machine. | Plumbing fittings and valves, ornaments. |
| Bronze | Copper containing up to 10% tin. | Yellowish brown in colour, resistant to corrosion, hard, tough and easy to machine. | Gears, springs and statues. |

Car parts such as engines, alloy wheels, exhausts, brake and suspension parts, all use different types of metals and alloys.

## Quick Test

1. Aluminium alloys have been used to replace steel in the production of many modern bicycle frames.

   **(a)** Describe what is meant by the term alloy.

   **(b)** Write 3 specification statements that would support the use of an aluminium alloy in the production of a bike frame.

   **(c)** What problem could be caused by using a ferrous metal in the production of a bike frame?

**Answers: 1. (a)** A pure metal mixed with another metal or element in order to improve the pure metal's properties. **(b)** Light weight, durable and resistant to corrosion. **(c)** Ferrous metals are prone to rusting if they are not finished properly.

# Plastics

## Types of plastic

Plastics were developed to replace or improve natural materials such as wood and metal. There are many different types of plastics with a wide range of properties and characteristics suitable for many applications. Plastics are all man-made, some from natural substances such as trees, plants, animals and insects. These are known as **natural** plastics; and include formaldehyde, shellac, cellulose and latex.

Most plastics are made from chemicals extracted from oil, coal or gas. The process is known as cracking and produces single molecules called monomers. A process called polymerisation then links thousands of monomers together to form polymers. These are known as synthetic plastics; and include acrylic, polystyrene, nylon and P.V.C.

There are two basic types of plastic, **thermoplastic** and **thermosetting** plastic.

Thermosetting

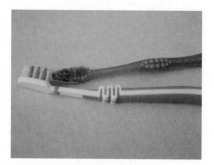

Thermoplastic

Plastics are available in a range of different forms, from powders and granules to sheets, rods and tubes. They can be easy to shape and their general properties of lightness of weight, water-resistance and low conductivity makes them a versatile material for use in the school workshop.

## Thermoplastics

**Thermoplastic** is a term given to plastic that can be shaped when heated. It will retain its shape and harden when cooled. If the plastic is then reheated it will return to its original shape, unless it has become damaged by overheating or overstretching. Its ability to return to its original shape is referred to as **plastic memory**.

| Name | Properties | Uses |
|------|-----------|------|
| Acrylic | Hard, brittle and easily scratched. Available in a range of colours and clear sheets. Is easy to machine and finish. | Signs, lighting reflectors and lenses. |
| Polystyrene | Light, buoyant and water-resistant. | Packaging, insulation and containers. |
| Nylon | Tough, durable and self-lubricating. | Clothing, gears, bearings and bristles. |
| P.V.C. | Stiff, water-resistant and durable. | Bottles, pipes and window frames. |

# Thermosetting

**Thermosetting** is the name given to plastic that can be shaped when heated the first time but when cooled will become permanently stiff and solid. It has no plastic memory and therefore cannot be reshaped.

| Name | Properties | Uses |
|------|-----------|------|
| Melamine formaldehyde | Scratch resistant, waterproof and odourless. | Kitchen worktops, furniture and shop fittings. |
| Urea formaldehyde | Hard, brittle with good insulation properties. | Electrical fittings, light switches and plugs. |
| Polyester resin | Can be laminated and formed without heat or pressure. | Boats, canoes and car body panels. |

# Acrylic

Acrylic is the most widely used plastic in schools. It is a thermoplastic with a number of properties useful for craft projects.

Acrylic

- is lightweight and durable
- is water resistant
- comes in a range of colours
- is easy to shape and form
- is easy to finish
- comes in a range of thicknesses and forms.

However, acrylic is brittle, which makes it likely to crack if care is not taken when cutting or drilling.

It is covered with a protective covering, as it is easy to scratch. This makes marking out difficult and often requires the use of templates or masking tape.

Protective polythene coating

**Top Tip**
It is important to finish the edges of acrylic before it is bent or formed. Once it is bent into shape it may become difficult to hold and more likely to break.

## Quick Test

1. Initially plastics were developed as a substitute for natural materials. There are now many different plastics with a wide range of properties.
   (a) Name three products that would not exist if plastic had not been invented.
   (b) For one of the examples given above, explain why it would not have existed before the invention of plastic.
   (c) Can plastic be considered a sustainable resource?
2. An advantage of using acrylic is that it has a plastic memory.
   (a) Describe what is meant by a plastic memory.
   (b) Describe how to polish the edges of acrylic.
   (c) Should the acrylic be bent before finishing the edges? Explain your answer.

**Answers: 1. (a)** Any products that have been manufactured in plastic (e.g. computer cases, mobile phones, games consoles) which have complex intricate forms which would have been difficult to make from natural materials. **(b)** For example, an electric iron's plug is mostly hard electrically-insulating plastic: its power-lead is also protected by insulating plastic and its body is made of waterproof, heat-insulating plastic. Without these plastics, such irons could not be made. **(c)** Plastics are not considered sustainable because they are produced from oil. However, they do lend themselves to recycling. **2. (a)** Plastic memory refers to a plastic's ability to return to its original shape when reheated. **(b)** 1. draw file, 2. wet and dry paper, 3. polish and buff with cloth or paper towel. **(c)** The edges of acrylic should be finished before bending or forming into shape. Polishing the edges before makes the process of polishing quicker; it is easier to hold in a vice and is less likely to snap.

# Manufactured boards

## Wide applications

Manufactured boards are used extensively now in the design and manufacture of many items of furniture. Historically much more traditional materials were used, with timber being the most popular choice of many craftsmen. Developments in manufacturing techniques and new glues and resins have brought about lots of new materials which offer the designer opportunities to design products that previously were not possible. Wide, thin sheets of material which are strong, rigid and robust are more common now, and new types continue to be developed. You will be familiar with some of the more traditional manufactured boards such as plywood, hardboard, blockboard, chipboard and MDF. These have been around for some time now and can be found in most homes, offices, restaurants and leisure facilities. Each of these boards offers advantages over solid timber and, when covered in natural veneers, can look just as good.

### Plywood

Plywood is made from layers or plies of wood which are glued together, the grain of each layer running at right angles and in the opposite direction to the next. This gives plywood the appearance of light and dark stripes on each of its edges. These glued layers make the plywood very strong and prevent it from twisting or warping. There is always an odd number of layers meaning that the grain in the outside pieces run the same way. This is why plywood can be referred to as 3-ply or 5-ply and so on.

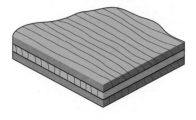

### Hardboard

This is an inexpensive material which is very thin and versatile. It is made by mixing wood fibres with water and a synthetic resin glue. It is then heated and compressed into a large, thin sheet, usually around 3 mm thick. Hardboard has one textured face and one smooth face which can be painted. It is not a very strong material and can be broken easily by hand.

## Blockboard

This is made by gluing strips of softwood together and then sandwiching them between two thin facings. This creates a strong, rigid board which is quite heavy. The exterior faces of the blockboard are usually veneered to give an attractive finish.

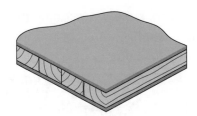

## Chipboard

Chipboard is made by gluing wood particles from waste and offcuts, then mixing them with resins before compressing them together. The board that is created lacks any real strength and some of the particles and chips can break off. It is very unattractive if left in this state, and its surface is usually covered by gluing a plastic laminate to it to enhance its appearance.

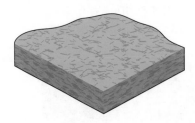

## Medium Density Fibreboard (MDF)

MDF is a composite material that has become more widely used by furniture makers and interior designers over recent years. Fine wood fibres are bonded together under heat and pressure with an adhesive. It is available in a range of thicknesses and has a smooth finish. It is a very strong material which does not warp.

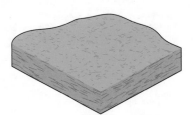

**Top Tip**
Thin boards of MDF and plywood offer strength and a rigidity that a similar size of solid wood does not. Manufactured boards are very useful for large panels and wide surfaces as they are flat and do not warp.

## Quick Test

1. Give two reasons why interior designers are likely to use manufactured boards for making counters and table tops.

2. Write down two properties of plywood.

**Answers: 1.** (i) the boards are flat and rigid and will not warp. They come in long wide sheets making them suitable for counter top. **2.** (i) flexible and able to be formed to give curved surfaces. (ii) thin but very strong.

# The woodwork lathe

The woodwork lathe is a machine that can be used to turn square sections of wood into cylinders and other more complex solids of revolution. Before this process begins the wood has to be prepared and made ready for turning.

## Preparing a blank for turning between centres

**Top Tip**
Don't use a ruler to measure the diameter of any part of your work. Outside callipers and vernier callipers are much more accurate.

Draw diagonal lines with a ruler and pencil to mark the centre on both ends of the wood.

Use a compass to construct an octagon on one end of the wood.

Use a marking gauge to draw parallel lines down each side of the wood.

Centre punch both ends of the wood to locate centres.

Use a tenon saw to cut a slot for the driving fork.

Use a smoothing plane to remove the corners of the wood before turning to a cylinder.

## Identifying the parts

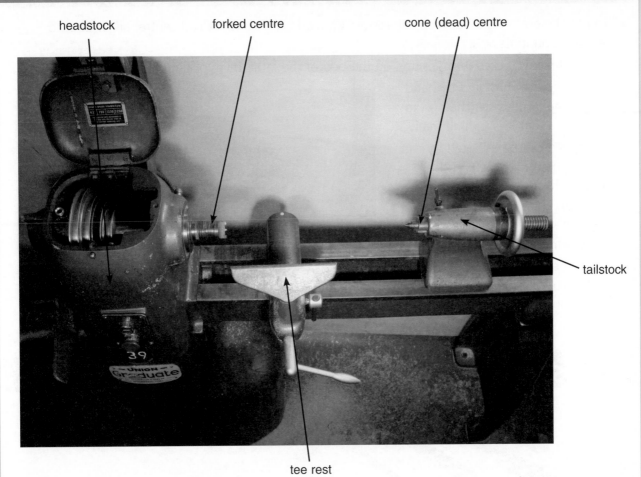

headstock     forked centre     cone (dead) centre

tailstock

tee rest

- The **headstock** houses the motor, pulleys and controls.
- The **tailstock** is used to slide along the bed of the lathe. It houses the dead centre which is used to support the workpiece.
- The **tee rest** is used to rest the turning tool on whilst turning. Its height can be adjusted to allow the tool to be used either on or above the centre axis of the workpiece.
- The **forked centre** is held in the headstock and then located in the groove sawn into the end of the workpiece. It grips into the end grain of the wood allowing it to drive the workpiece round.
- The **cone (dead) centre** is used to support the workpiece by positioning it in the centre of the punched hole at the end of the workpiece and tightening the tailstock into position.

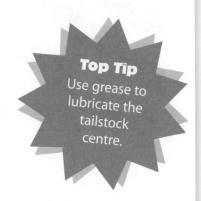

**Top Tip**
Use grease to lubricate the tailstock centre.

## The set-up

- The workpiece is held between centres by a forked centre and a dead centre, allowing it to revolve around its axis.
- The tool rest is locked into position on the bed of the lathe by a locking handle.
- The workpiece is rotated by hand before the lathe is switched on to make sure that it is turning freely.
- The speed can be adjusted by moving the pulley belt. (This should always be done by a teacher). The speed of the lathe will depend on the diameter of the work being turned.
- It may be necessary to put grease on the cone of the dead centre to stop it burning the wood.

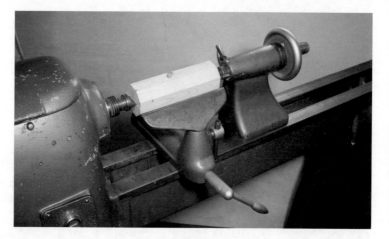

## Tools

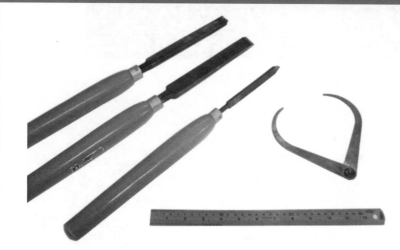

Tools used in turning

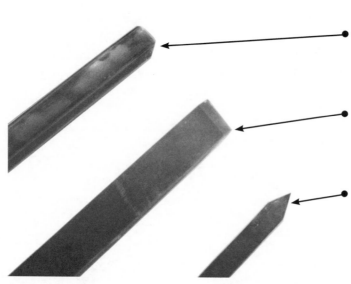

- The **gouge** is the most frequently used turning tool. It is usually the first tool to be used when turning a new workpiece to a cylinder.
- The **skew chisel** is useful when trying to get a good surface finish on the cylinder. It can also be used to cut grooves and conical shapes.
- The **parting chisel** is used to cut shoulders and steps and for parting off work.

## Safety

- Goggles must be worn at all times when working on the lathe.
- Long hair, loose clothing and jewellery should be made safe.
- Check that the workpiece has been held securely and that the tool rest and tailstock are locked.
- Turn the workpiece by hand before switching on to ensure that it clears the tool rest.

**Top Tip**

The wood may eventually heat up, smoke and make a screeching noise. This is caused by the friction of the wood turning and rubbing against the metal cone of the dead centre. Add a smear of grease to the tip of the dead centre to lubricate it and make sure that the work piece is held tightly between both centres.

## Processes

Various cylindrical forms can be created by turning between centres using the wood lathe. Before any shaping can be done, the wood must be turned down to a cylinder to allow it to turn true.

- The gouge is used for general cutting to create true cylinders, hollows or spools. Remember that it is important to maintain the correct angle for cutting with the handle pointing towards the floor.
- The skew chisel is used for planing to create chamfers, v-cuts and beads.
- The parting chisel is used for cutting shoulders and parting off.

shoulder
bobbin
chamfer
v-cuts
hollow
spool

### Roughing down

Using a gouge, make a direct cut away from the headstock.

### Planning

Using the skew chisel on the lathe.

### Parting

The parting chisel is being used on the lathe.

## Quick Test

1. Describe in sequence the stages involved in preparing a piece of timber before turning on the lathe.

2. State two checks that should be carried out on the lathe before switching on.

3. Why should the length of the workpiece be longer than the required size of the finished part?

**Answers: 1.** Draw diagonal lines on both ends of the workpiece. Draw a circle on both ends. Cut a 2 mm deep groove along one of the diagonal lines on one end. Centre punch the middle of the other end. Plane the corners of the workpiece to give an octagonal length of timber. **2.** Check that the work does not hit the tool rest and can turn freely. Check that the workpiece is held securely between centres. **3.** The ends of the workpiece will get damaged by the forked centre and the dead centre. The additional length will allow new shoulders to be cut on the lathe.

# Drills

## Types and uses

Drilling is a process for creating circular holes in wood, metal or plastic. It requires a drill and a drill bit. The type of drill and drill bit depends on the type of material being drilled and the size of hole required. Drills can be powered mechanically or by hand. The pillar drill or pedestal drill is a mechanical drill, where your work is placed on a table and the drill is brought down using a handle.

## The pillar drill

The pillar drill has a number of different parts.

- The head consists of the motor together with the pulleys, on/off switch, feed handle, chuck, depth gauge and quill lock.
- The table can be adjusted by sliding it up and down the pillar. This allows different sizes of material to be drilled.
- The base is bolted to the workshop floor to give greater stability.
- The table provides a flat surface on which to place your work. Work would usually be held in a hand vice or a machine vice.
- The chuck is where the drill bits are held. The chuck can be loosened, tightened and adjusted using a chuck key in order to hold a range of different drill bits.

**Top Tip**
When drilling a through hole in wood or acrylic always remember to drill into a scrap piece of wood. This will ensure a clean hole is created in the wood and limits the chances of the acrylic cracking.

## Speed

The pillar drill can be set to different speeds using the v-belt and pulleys, which work in a similar way to the gears on a bike. In general, the smaller the drill bit used, the faster the speed should be, and the larger the drill bit used, the slower the speed should be.

Select the correct speed

# The chuck

The chuck used in the pillar drill has three jaws which can be opened and closed using a chuck key. Turning the key to the left (anticlockwise) loosens the chuck while turning it right (clockwise) tightens the chuck. The chuck is protected by a chuck guard – this stops anything coming into contact with the chuck accidently when it is in motion.

# Depth gauge

The pillar drill has a depth gauge which allows blind holes to be drilled accurately. The depth gauge can be adjusted by loosening it, pulling the drill bit down with the feed handle to the required length and tightening the gauge. The feed handle can now only be pulled down as far as the depth stop.

**Top Tip**
A blind hole is a hole that only reaches a certain depth, i.e. it is not drilled through.

# Safety

Before using the pillar drill a number of precautions and checks are required. Before switching the drill on check that:

- the drill bit is secure in the centre of the three-jaw chuck;
- the drill is set at the correct speed;
- the chuck key has been removed;
- the chuck guard is in place;
- the workpiece is held firmly in place.

# Other types of drills

It is not always possible or convenient to use the pillar drill. The material may be too big, awkward or heavy to fit under the pillar drill. There is a range of hand tools that can be used to cut holes in different materials.

The cordless drill is powered by a rechargeable battery. Cordless drills have forward and reverse gears and a torque setting which allows them to be used as power screwdrivers. The size of the chuck limits the diameter of drill that can be used.

A hand drill can be used to drill pilot holes and other small holes.

A hand brace can be used to drill larger diameter holes when it is not practical to use the pillar drill. It is used together with an auger bit which has a specially designed tapered shank.

## Quick Test

**1.** What set should you use on the pillar drill when drilling a blind hole?

**2.** When would it be necessary to change the speed of the pillar drill?

**3.** When drilling a hole through acrylic what precautions should be taken to prevent it from cracking?

**Answers: 1.** Depth gauge. **2.** When using larger diameter holes or drilling into different materials. **3.** Covering with marking tape, checking drill set to correct speed and ensuring the acrylic is supported on a piece of scrap wood.

# The mortice machine

## Cutting mortices

The mortice machine drills **square holes** to cut a mortice. The square hole is cut using a special **mortice bit** held in the machine head. The mortice bit is made of an auger bit fitted inside a square-edged chisel. The auger bit cuts a round hole and the chisel cuts the square corners. There are various sizes of mortice bit available to cut different mortice widths. Different lengths of mortice can be cut using the **movable bed** and the hand wheel. The mortice machine can be set to cut different depths using the **depth stop**. Using the depth stop ensures the bottom of the mortice is level and accurate.

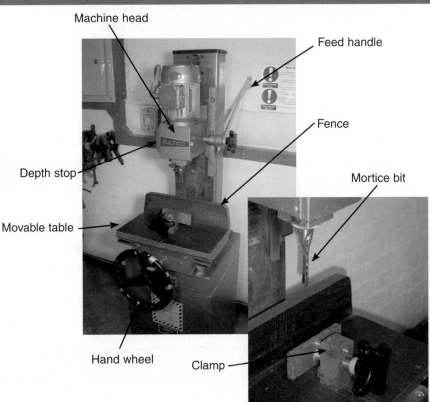

Machine head
Feed handle
Fence
Mortice bit
Depth stop
Movable table
Hand wheel
Clamp

## Using the mortice machine

- Mark the position of the mortice on the workpiece using a mortice gauge.
- Use the clamp to hold the workpiece securely against the fence and the bed.
- Use the hand wheel to align the mortice bit with the mortice to be cut.
- Set the depth stop to the required depth.
- Use the lever to begin cutting the mortice, moving the hand wheel to obtain the required length.

## Safety

- Set the machine only when it is switched off.
- Make sure the workpiece is secure.
- When drilling a through mortice, a scrap piece of wood must be placed under the workpiece.
- Wear goggles.

## Quick Questions

1. Name the chisel that would be used to cut a mortice by hand.
2. How would you make sure that the mortice bit did not overheat when cutting a deep mortice?

**Answers: 1.** Mortice chisel. **2.** Cut to the depth in stages, rather than in one go.

# Sanders

## A machine for finishing

During your course it is likely that you will have experienced using a sander similar to the one shown. This is a useful machine for finishing off the surfaces and ends of wood, whether they are flat or rounded. It is not a shaping or cutting machine and should only be used to remove small amounts of material.

## The disc

The disc sander should be used to sand the end grain on wood. The sander rotates clockwise so it is important that you use only the right-hand side of the disc so that the dust produced is taken down into the extractor. It is obvious that if the left-hand side was used, dust would be blown up into the air. You should not press the wood too hard against the disc otherwise the surface being sanded will burn.

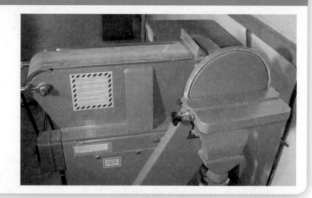

## The belt

The belt on the sander is used to sand along the grain of the wood. As the name suggests, there is a continuous belt of sandpaper which is mounted on two rotating drums. Your workpiece should be pressed gently down on top of the belt and should rest up against the stop at the end of the machine. Again, this allows dust to be taken down into the extractor.

## Safety

As with any machine you should not use the sander until you have been shown how, and even then you should not switch it on without the permission of your teacher.

- Ask permission before you use the machine.
- Always wear goggles.
- Tuck in any loose clothing that may get caught, and remove loose jewellery.
- Do not talk to anyone whilst you are using the machine.
- Do not misbehave or allow anyone else to misbehave near you when you are using the machine.
- Always switch the machine off after you have used it.

**Top Tip**
The sander is for finishing, not for cutting or shaping material. You should only sand small amounts off your wood and you should always work accurately to a line.

## Quick Test

1. What should you do to avoid burning the end grain of a piece of wood when using the disc sander?

**Answers: 1.** Apply only light pressure to the wood.

# The band saw

## Use with care

This is a machine that you should only use under the direct supervision of your teacher. It may be that your teacher prefers that you do not use it at all. He or she may choose to demonstrate how it works. In any case, it is very dangerous and should be operated with care no matter who is operating it.

Band saws are very useful for cutting long straight lines and gentle curves on wood or manufactured board.

## Safety

- Always wear safety goggles when using these machines.
- Ask your teacher to check and adjust the guards if necessary before switching on.
- Keep your fingers away from the blade.
- Do not misbehave or allow anyone to misbehave near you.
- Remove loose jewellery and tuck in loose clothing.
- Always switch the machine off after use.

**Top Tip**

Always keep your fingers away from the cutting line of the band saw. It is preferable to place one hand either side of the blade but well away from its cutting edge.

## Quick Test

1. Write down one safety check that should be made on a band saw before switching it on.

**Answers: 1.** Make sure that the guard is lowered to the minimum height necessary to cut the material.

# Jigsaws

## Types and uses

The jigsaw is particularly good for tight curves and small intricate work and, as its name suggests, jigsaw-sized shapes. The machine is electrically powered and raises and lowers a thin blade in a reciprocating action while work is pushed slowly through it.

There are two different types of jigsaw commonly used in the workshop:

- the fixed jigsaw
- the portable jigsaw.

## Fixed jigsaw

These jigsaws can be **bench mounted** or **free-standing**. They are fitted with a **fine blade** that makes them suitable for cutting **curves** and **intricate shapes** in thin sheet materials such as MDF, plywood and acrylic.

The blade is moved up and down mechanically. The shape is achieved by guiding the material through the saw. Care must be taken when using this machine as the blades can break easily. A light even pressure will achieve the best results.

The jigsaw is fitted with a **shoe** to stop the material vibrating or chattering. This allows more accurate cutting. When setting the shoe, the material must still be able to slide freely through the saw.

The blade from the jigsaw can be removed to allow internal shapes to be cut. This requires holes to be drilled first, to allow access to the shape. When the blade is replaced it must be set to the correct tension before it is used.

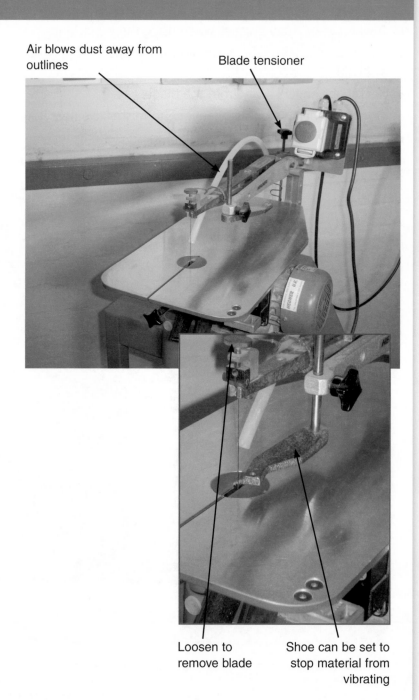

Air blows dust away from outlines

Blade tensioner

Loosen to remove blade

Shoe can be set to stop material from vibrating

# Portable jigsaw

These portable jigsaws are fitted with a thicker, more robust blade. They can be used to cut complex curves in larger thicker sheet material. The blade again moves up and down but this time the saw itself is moved to cut the desired shape. The material should be clamped to a bench and care must be taken to ensure that the blade can more freely without cutting the bench or the power cord. All new jigsaws are fitted with a guard and a dust bag. Again, these saws can be used to cut internal shapes by first drilling a hole slightly bigger than the saw blade to allow access.

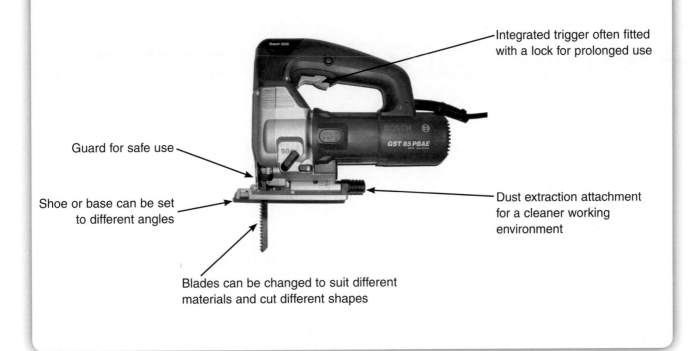

Integrated trigger often fitted with a lock for prolonged use

Guard for safe use

Shoe or base can be set to different angles

Dust extraction attachment for a cleaner working environment

Blades can be changed to suit different materials and cut different shapes

## Quick Test

1. Describe how to set the shoe correctly on the fixed jigsaw.

2. List three checks you would make on the jigsaw before switching it on.

**Answers: 1. Place the material to be cut on the table of the jig saw, loosen and lower the shoe until it touches the surface of the material, ensure the material will slide smoothly between the shoe and table, tighten the shoe in place. 2. Work to be cut is securely held in place, the blade is free to move, the blade and cable are positioned so that the cable can't be cut.**

# Laminating

## Methods and uses

Laminating is a method of producing shapes that would be difficult or expensive to cut from solid material such as the frames of bent wood furniture. It can also be used to create materials with greater lengths, widths or depths – many wooden table tops are created in this way. The properties of materials can also be improved by laminating, e.g. plastic laminates on kitchen worktops make them waterproof and easy to clean.

## Creating a bend in wood

Suitable woods for bending are **plywood, ash, birch, beech**.

### Formers

To create the desired shape, thin strips of wood are layered together with glue and bent around a **former**. Once the glue sets the layers of wood are held together, stopping them from springing back to their natural form. Various woods up to 3 mm thick can be bent. It is sometimes necessary to dampen the wood to make it more flexible.

### Solid formers

For small items a **solid former** can be cut from a block of wood. The shape required will be cut through the middle of a block. The thickness of the finished object must be taken into account. The laminates can then be placed between the two halves of the former and cramped together. Any excess glue should be removed to stop the laminate from sticking to the former.

For larger shapes it may be necessary to construct a frame to bend the laminates around.

### Vacuum press

Laminated shapes can also be created using a **vacuum press**. This has the advantage of requiring only one half of the former. The vacuum bag draws the wooden laminates around a former instead of clamping.

# Laminating boards using sash cramps

Laminating sections of wood together will create boards that are more stable and less likely to **warp**. Sections of wood are cut to the required length and thickness. The sections of wood are then glued and cramped together using **sash cramps**. The sections of timber should be arranged so that the grain alternates to provide a more stable material. Care should be taken to protect the edges of the material when using the sash cramps and all excess glue must be wiped off.

Sash cramps positioned top and bottom prevent material bowing

Check sections are flush as cramps are tightened

Scrap material to prevent bruising the edge of the material

# Plastic laminates

Plastic laminates can be used to improve the properties of some man-made boards. Gluing a plastic sheet, such as formica, to chipboard creates an attractive, durable and waterproof surface. When gluing plastic laminates, a contact adhesive must be used in a well ventilated area.

**Top Tip**

It is likely that the timber sections will move as they are being cramped. Take the time at this stage to ensure they are aligned correctly before the glue sets. This will create flat boards that require less preparation and finishing.

## Quick Test

1. Why is the wood sometimes dampened before laminating?
2. What must be taken into account when designing a former for laminating wood?
3. What is the advantage of constructing furniture, such as tables and chairs, from laminated forms?

**Answers: 1.** Dampening the wood makes it softer, more pliable and easier to bend into shape. **2.** The thickness of the material to be formed into shape. **3.** Less construction, fewer joints and less material waste. It can also provide more stable board materials which are less likely to warp.

# Joining wood

## Selecting joints

There are a large number of different woodwork joints that can be used to construct a project. The type chosen will depend on a number of factors such as:

- the type of material being used
- the strength required of the joint
- the direction of the force applied
- the aesthetic look of the project
- the quantity to be produced.

In general, woodwork joints can be split into two categories: frame or carcase. Each joint differs in strength and complexity. Often, the more complex the joint, the stronger it will be.

## Care with joints

Great care and attention should be taken when marking out and cutting a joint. Accuracy is so important that specialised tools have been developed to ensure a good fit, e.g. mortice gauge, sliding bevel, marking knife, mortice chisel and rebate plane.

**Top Tip**
Always hatch the waste and cut to the waste side of the line: the finished joint is only as good as the marking out.

## Frame joints

Frame joints are used to join sections of timber in such items as tables and chairs. Carcase joints are used when constructing projects from sheet material, such as kitchen units and wardrobes. The frame joints used most commonly in the school workshop are:

- mortice and tenon
- lap joint
- rub joint
- halving joint
- dowel joint.

### Mortice and tenon

A traditional joint commonly used for both frame and carcase construction. If cut accurately, it provides a very strong joint that can be cut as a stopped or through joint.

### Lap joint

Traditionally used to join at a corner, it provides a stronger and more attractive joint than a butt joint.

### Rub (butt) joint

A simple joint mainly used when strip gluing boards. It is essential that a good surface contact is created through flat square edges.

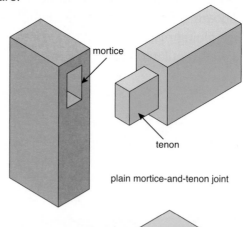

mortice

tenon

plain mortice-and-tenon joint

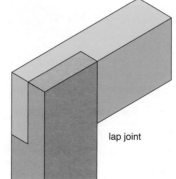

lap joint

## Halving joint

An attractive, strong frame joint that produces a flush finish. Each section of timber has a section of wood removed and then interlocked.

## Dowel joint

A simple joint often used in place of more complex joints. Commonly used in the manufacture of flat-pack furniture. Accuracy is essential when drilling the holes for the dowel, often requiring a dowelling jig.

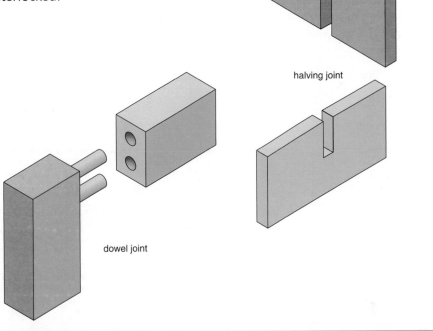

halving joint

dowel joint

# Carcase joints

The carcase joints used most commonly in the school workshop are:

- rebate joint
- housing joint
- dowel joint.

## Rebate joint

Similar to a lap joint but used to join the corners of sheet material. One of the pieces of material is cut to cover the end of the other to provide a more attractive joint.

## Housing joint

There are two common types of housing joint; stopped or through. Both are used as a traditional method of constructing shelving. The more complex stopped housing joint is used to create a more attractive front face to the shelving.

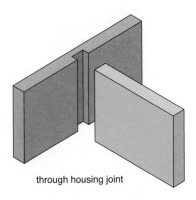

through housing joint

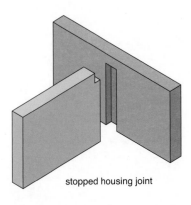

stopped housing joint

## Assembly

After woodwork joints have been cut they will have to be put together and held in place. Applying pressure improves the bond between the two parts being joined. It is good practice to dry-cramp before gluing. Dry cramping is a term used for assembling the project without glue in order to check the fit, accuracy and placement of cramps etc. During the final assembly, it is important to check for squareness and winding.

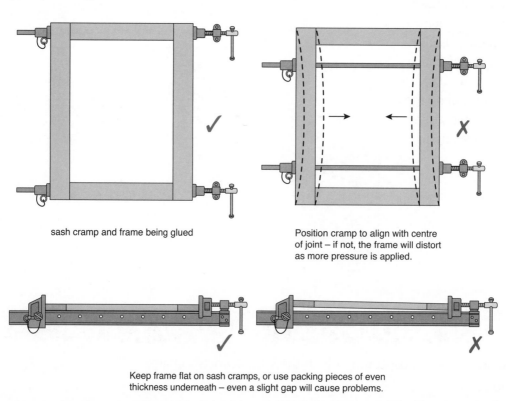

sash cramp and frame being glued

Position cramp to align with centre of joint – if not, the frame will distort as more pressure is applied.

Keep frame flat on sash cramps, or use packing pieces of even thickness underneath – even a slight gap will cause problems.

## Knockdown fittings

Knockdown fittings have been created to replace time consuming, traditional woodwork joints. The mass production of furniture often requires simple methods of construction and assembly. Knockdown fittings also allow self-assembly of furniture as they require no specialised tools or equipment. Self-assembly makes furniture affordable and easy to transport.

# Metal turning

## The centre lathe

The centre lathe is a machine that is used primarily to make cylindrical forms. It can be used to do many other things, but at Standard Grade you will only be required to know the basics of metal turning. It is likely that you have seen or used common processes such as **facing**, **parallel turning**, **taper turning**, **knurling** and **drilling** during your course. You should be knowledgeable about the parts of the lathe and be able to set it up, ready for use.

## Preparation

It is important that before you use the metalwork lathe, the cutting tool is set to cutting height and checked. The photograph opposite shows this being done using the centre point of the live centre.

It is also necessary to check that the lathe is set to the correct speed for the material you are cutting and the process you are using. The speed can be adjusted using the levers on the headstock.

## Safety

Probably the most complex machine you will use in the workshop, the metalwork lathe is safe if used properly and sensibly.

- Goggles must be worn at all times.
- Loose clothing and jewellery must be removed and hair must be tied back.
- You must select the correct speed for whatever process you are carrying out.
- You must never touch the metal shavings, called swarf, with your bare hands.
- The workpiece must be held securely in the three-jaw chuck.
- You must never allow yourself to be distracted whilst using the lathe.
- Ask your teacher to check your lathe set-up before switching it on.
- Switch the machine off if it begins to make any unusual noises.

**Top Tip**
When checking the tool height you may find it easier to gently sandwich a metal rule between the cutting tool and the length of a bar held in the chuck. If it stands vertically then the cutting tool is at the correct height.

# Identifying the parts

The **headstock** houses the motor, gears and controls.

The **saddle or carriage** is a base unit on which the cross slide, compound slide and tool post are mounted. It straddles the bed-ways rather like the saddle on a horse and can be moved along the whole length by hand control or automatic feed.

The **apron** is the front part of the saddle upon which are mounted hand controls.

The **tailstock** can slide along the bed-ways of the lathe. It is used to house the live centre and Jacob's chuck.

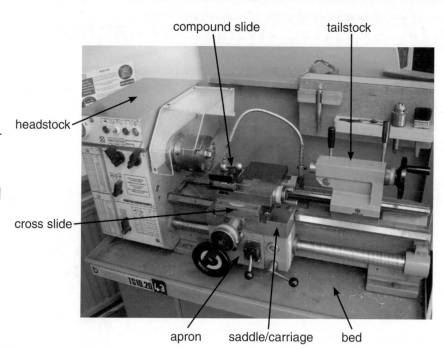

The **bed** of the lathe is the base of the lathe and normally it is made from cast iron. The bed-ways and headstock are mounted on the bed.

The **cross slide** is mounted on top of the saddle and is used when facing the end of the material.

The **compound slide** is mounted on top of the cross slide and can be set to many angles. It is used for taper turning and chamfering.

# Processes

- Facing is usually the first process to be carried out. The end of the metal bar is 'squared off'. This reduces the length of the bar and if the cutting tool is not set to centre height it will leave a small 'pip' on the end of the bar.

- Parallel turning is shown here. It is used to clean up the length of the bar and reduce its diameter. This can be done manually by hand or using the automatic feed.

- Taper turning and chamfering is done by setting the compound slide to the required angle then operating it by hand.

- Knurling is used to add texture to the surface of the workpiece. A knurling tool is used and the speed of the lathe is reduced.

**Top Tip**
Remember to select the correct speed of the lathe when drilling large diameter holes and knurling. Ask your teacher to recommend the best speed for this operation.

- Drilling a hole in the end of the bar can be done by first using a centre drill, shown opposite. The centre drill is held in a Jacob's chuck which in turn is held in the tailstock. The centre drill can then be replaced by a twist drill of the required size to drill the hole. The hole created by the centre drill will give the twist drill a good location and stop it from wandering.

**Top Tip**
If you are drilling a hole bigger than 6 mm then you should do it in two stages. For example, if the hole you require is 10 mm then drill a 5mm hole first.

- The centre drill can also be used to drill a tapered hole that allows a live centre to be inserted and used to support the workpiece.

## Quick Test

**1.** Why is it necessary for the end of the live centre to rotate?

**2.** What safety precaution must be observed when using a metalwork lathe with regard to swarf?

**Answers: 1.** To avoid the metal workpiece grinding on the centre and causing a build up of friction and heat on the two parts. **2.** Swarf should never be picked up with bare hands.

# Casting aluminium

## Sand-casting

Sand-casting is a process used to make complex metal forms. The process involves pouring molten metal into moulds made in 'green' moulding sand using a pattern. When the metal cools and solidifies it can be removed from the sand. 'Green' sand is the name given to damp sand (which holds its shape). Water is used as the binding agent. Oil-bound sand can also be used to cut down on preparation time.

## Making the pattern

A pattern has to be made to create the mould cavity. Close-grained hardwoods, softwoods and MDF are popular as they are easy to shape and give a good surface finish.

Rounded corners, tapered sides and a smooth surface will allow the pattern to be removed easily and ensure a good quality casting.

**Top Tip**
Patterns should be made slightly larger to compensate for casting shrinkage.

A good pattern will have:
- a flat back
- tapered sides
- radius corners
- a smooth surface finish

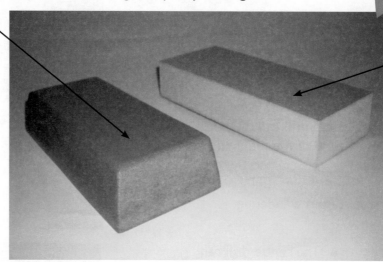

Pattern not suitable for creating mould.

## Safety precautions

Pouring aluminium can be a hazardous process and specialised safety equipment needs to be worn.
- Visor should be worn to protect not just the eyes but the whole face.
- Gauntlets should be worn to protect the hands and forearms.
- A leather apron should be worn to protect clothing.
- Leather footwear should be worn to protect feet.

**Top Tip**
When packing the moulding box with the rammer, avoid packing the sand too tight as this will make removing the pattern and sprue pins difficult.

## Making the mould

### Equipment

Creating a mould requires specialised equipment, which is shown below.

The drag forms the bottom of the moulding box.

The cope is the top of the moulding box.

Parting powder is used to ensure the two halves of the moulding box separate and the pattern does not stick to the sand.

Green moulding sand or sand mixed with oil is used in casting.

Sprue pins are tapered pins used to create the runner and the riser.

A riddle is used to remove the lumps in the moulding sand.

A rammer is used to compact the moulding sand around the pattern.

Bellows used to blow away loose sand.

Place the drag upside down and position the pattern.

Cover the pattern and the bottom of the drag with parting powder.

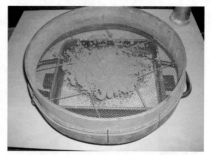

Sift the moulding sand over the pattern using a riddle to create facing sand.

Ram in backing sand and smooth off excess.

Use rammer to compact sand.

Strickle off drag to create a flat bottom before turning the drag over.

Locate the cope on top of the drag, then place sprue pins close to the pattern in a position to ensure a good flow of aluminium.

Fill cope with riddled sand, compact with rammer and create pouring basins, then remove sprue pins.

Open the moulding box, remove the pattern and cut in-gate and out-gate. Use bellows to gently blow away loose sand. Then re-close the moulding box.

**Pouring basins** – allow aluminium to be poured into the runner and indicate when riser is full without the risk of spilling.

**In-gate** – allows molten aluminium into the mould cavity.

**Out-gate** – allows molten aluminium and gasses out of the cavity.

# Casting the aluminium

Aluminium is used in school workshops as it has a relatively low melting temperature. It is heated in a crucible until molten. The aluminium should be preheated to avoid the risk of condensation. Once the aluminium is molten a de-gassing tablet may be used to remove any impurities in the metal.

This is typical of the kind of crucible used in schools to heat the aluminium.

When the aluminium is molten the moulding box should be placed in a casting tray, close to the crucible. The molten aluminium should then be poured into the runner allowing it to flow through the in-gate and filling the mould cavity. The mould is full when the molten aluminium can be seen in the riser.

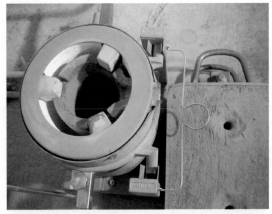

Once the aluminium has solidified the casting can be removed using tongs and allowed to cool. After cooling, the aluminium from the runner and riser can be removed and the cast finished. This is known as fettling.

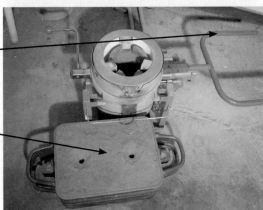

Handles used to pour aluminium.

Moulding box positioned next to the crucible.

## Safety checks

- Good ventilation (extraction on)
- Preheat aluminium
- Casting pit
- Vent holes above the pattern

## Quick Test

1. What makes aluminium suitable for casting in a school workshop?
2. What precautions should be taken before the aluminium is placed in the crucible?
3. The moulding box comes in two halves to allow the moulding cavity to be created.
   (a) State the name of the top and bottom of the moulding box.
   (b) What is used to make sure the top and bottom halves of the mould do not stick together?
4. State what is used to create the runner and riser.
5. Describe what the runner is used for.
6. Explain how you would know that the mould is full.

**Answers: 1.** It has a low melting point. **2.** The metal should be preheated. **3. (a)** drag and cope **(b)** parting powder **4.** sprue pins **5.** To pour the molten aluminium into the mould cavity **6.** Molten aluminium will be seen in the riser.

# Drilling metal

## Golden rules

Most of the holes that you will drill in metal will be done using a twist drill in the pillar drill similar to the set-up shown.

There are a few golden rules you should follow to ensure that the hole you drill is accurate and that you are safe.

- Centre punch the metal before drilling. This will give the twist drill an accurate location and stop it wandering.

- Don't hold the metal in your hand – it may slip out or get caught in the drill and spin around. Use a machine vice or hand vice.

- Be sure the drill is set to the correct speed. The belt on the pulleys of the pillar drill can be adjusted as shown in the photograph on page 42. The speed required will depend on the material that you are drilling and the size of hole. You should always check with your teacher.

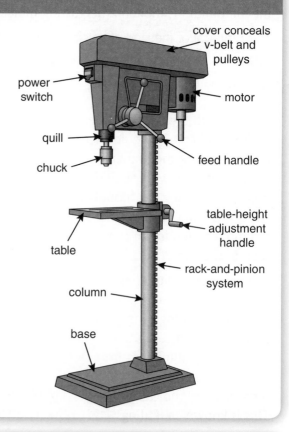

Labels: cover conceals v-belt and pulleys, power switch, motor, quill, chuck, feed handle, table-height adjustment handle, table, rack-and-pinion system, column, base

## Safety

- Goggles must always be worn when using the pillar drill.
- Do not touch the swarf produced with your bare hands.
- Remove loose clothing and jewellery and tie back loose hair.
- You must never allow yourself to be distracted when using the pillar drill.
- Do not have your hands too close to the drill and use a vice to hold the metal.

**Top Tip**
Set the depth stop if you are drilling a blind hole.

## Quick Test

**1.** After drilling sheet metal a 'burr' is often formed around the hole. What is a 'burr'?

**2.** Write a short note on how each of the following is used when drilling.
  **(a)** a machine vice
  **(b)** a hand vice

**Answers: 1.** A burr is a rough edge that is often formed on the underside of a hole after drilling metal. **2.** See descriptions on page 90.

# Cutting metal

Generally, the metals used in the craft room are harder than the woods and plastics. They are more resistant to cutting than these other materials and require specialised tools to shape them.

## Hacksaws

Hacksaws are specifically designed to make straight cuts in metal. They are used in the workshop to cut metal tubes, sheets and bars. There are two types – the hacksaw and the junior hacksaw.

### Hacksaw

The hacksaw's blade is held in a frame. This allows the blade to be adjusted to suit different purposes.

- The blade can be changed to suit different materials, i.e. hard materials require a fine blade and softer materials need a coarse blade.
- Different lengths of blade can be used.
- The angle of the blade can be changed to make cuts which are deeper than the frame of the saw.
- More than one blade can be inserted to cut thicker slots in the material.

To change or adjust the blade, the tensioning nut (thumbscrew) must be loosened. If the blade is to be set to a different angle, the blade pin and bolt must be rotated in the square hole housed in the handle.

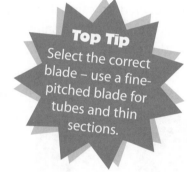

**Top Tip**
Select the correct blade – use a fine-pitched blade for tubes and thin sections.

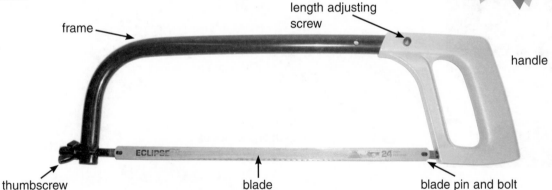

length adjusting screw

frame

handle

thumbscrew

blade

blade pin and bolt

### Junior hacksaw

The smaller of the two hacksaws, the junior hacksaw is used for cutting lighter material that requires smaller cuts or for where access with the hacksaw is difficult.

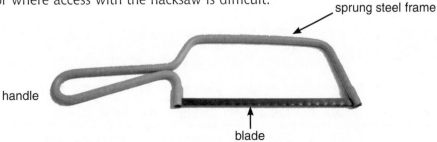

sprung steel frame

handle

blade

## Piercing saw and abrafile

These can be used to cut complex and intricate curved shapes in thin sheet metal. They have a toothed, circular blade which can be coarse, medium or fine.

Piercing saw

↑ Fine blade for intricate work

## Snips and shears

Tin snips are used to cut thin sheet metal. The two types commonly used in workshops are straight and curved tin snips. They can be held in an engineer's vice to give greater control and better leverage. Straight tin snips are used for cutting straight lines in thin sheet metal. Curved tin snips used for cutting curves in thin sheet metal.

Fixed in position, the shearing machine is used to cut sheets, rods and strips. Its lever produces greater forces and allows thicker material to be shaped.

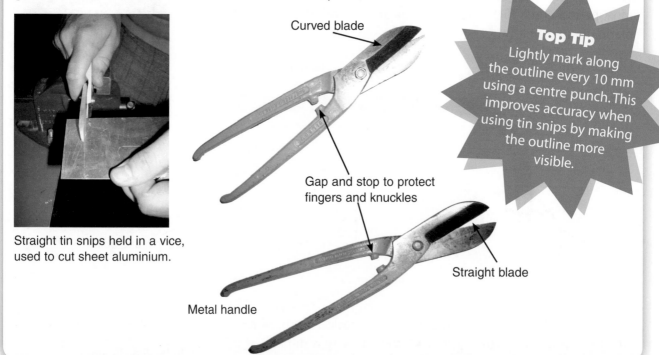

Curved blade

**Top Tip**
Lightly mark along the outline every 10 mm using a centre punch. This improves accuracy when using tin snips by making the outline more visible.

Gap and stop to protect fingers and knuckles

Straight tin snips held in a vice, used to cut sheet aluminium.

Straight blade

Metal handle

## Quick Test

1. State which hand tool would be used to cut aluminium tubing to the required length.

2. Describe what makes an abrafile suitable for cutting curves in metal.

Answers: 1. Hacksaw 2. The thin cylindrical blade allows it to cut on all surfaces.

# Heat treatments of metal

## Changing the properties of metals

The properties of a metal can be changed by heat treatments. Metal can be made softer or harder by heating it to a specific critical temperature and then having the speed at which it is allowed to cool controlled. The appearance of the metal will have changed very little as all of the changes will have occurred within its structure. The heat will cause molecules of metal to move around and change shape and cooling the metal will fix these molecules into a new structure, thereby giving the metal different working properties. Heat treatments are carried out using the forge and hearth.

**Top Tip**
When hardening a piece of steel, heat it to a cherry red colour then quench it in oil, brine or tepid water. It may crack if you quench it in cold water.

## Annealing

Most of us have experienced how easily a paper clip will break after it has been bent back and forward a few times. This is caused by stresses building up within the metal due to the work being done to it during the bending action. This is referred to as **work hardening**. These stresses can be relieved by a process called **annealing**. Aluminium is annealed by gently heating it and then allowing it to cool naturally. Aluminium is a soft metal which has a low melting point, and very little discolouration occurs when it is heated.

To avoid overheating aluminium, first cover it in soap; when the soap turns black or dark brown this indicates that the correct annealing temperature has been reached.

## Hardening

**Hardening** is a process that makes some steel very hard and brittle – often too brittle to be used without breaking or shattering. The tough properties of the metal can be brought back by tempering it after it has been hardened. Hardening is done by heating steel to a cherry red colour then quenching it quickly in tepid water. Quenching it in cold water may crack the steel. Rapid cooling is promoted by stirring the workpiece in the water.

# Tempering

**Tempering** is a process that relieves the steel of this extreme brittleness, making it a more useful and adaptable material. This process is carried out by cleaning the steel so that the tempering colours can be seen, then heating the steel to the required tempering colour before immediately quenching it in water. Increasing the tempering colour reduces the metal's brittleness and increases its toughness. There needs to be a compromise here and this will depend on what the finished steel is to be used for. Tempering colours start at a pale straw colour and move through an orange/brown to a dark purple then blue.

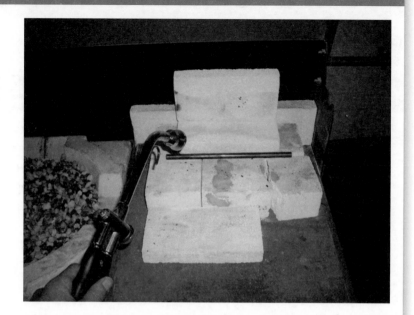

## Quick Test

1. What does annealing do to aluminium?
2. Name the process where a steel screwdriver blade is heated to cherry red then quenched in tepid water or oil.

**Answers: 1.** It makes the aluminium more malleable. **2.** Hardening.

# Joining metals

## Right joint, right job

There are various methods and processes used to join metal. Some are permanent and some semi-permanent. The method chosen depends on the individual project's function, the environment in which it is to be used, maintenance issues and cost. **Permanent processes** include welding, soldering, brazing and riveting, while **semi-permanent methods** include nuts and bolts, machine screws, pop-rivets and self-tapping screws.

### Welding

Welding is a process used to join two pieces of the same metal. The metal surfaces are heated until they are molten using an electric arc or an oxy-acetylene flame. A filler or welding rod is melted at the same time to create a pool of molten metal which solidifies to form the weld.

A flux is used to ensure that a strong weld is created, free from impurities and oxidisation. The flux can be a powder coating on the welding rod or can be in the form of a gas.

### Soldering

Soldering is a process that joins two pieces of metal using an alloy of tin and lead with a low melting point. The alloy or solder is heated using a soldering iron until molten. When it cools, it bonds the metal together. The base metal is raised to the same temperature as the solder's melting point.

The soldering iron is heated either on the forge or electrically. The bit of a soldering iron is made from copper so that it heats up easily.

Before soldering check that:

- surfaces are clean and a close fit
- flux is used
- surfaces are tinned (covered with a thin layer of solder).

### Brazing

Brazing also uses a metal alloy to join metal together. The difference is that the metal being joined is heated to melt the solder. Instead of a soldering iron, the metal is heated using the hearth torch and the solder melts as it touches the metal. The flux is applied to the metal and the end of the brazing rod.

### Spot-welding

Spot-welding can be used to fuse sheets of metal together. Heat is produced using electricity passed through two copper contacts or electrodes. The spot-welding machine can be set to suit different gauges of steel.

The electrodes and material must be clean to reduce the risk of sparks and ensure a good joint.

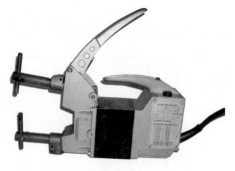

spot welder

# Riveting

A range of different rivets can be used, depending on the material or situation. Aluminium rivets are commonly used in school as they are easy to form, but brass, copper, and mild steel are also used.

| Snap or round head rivets | Countersunk head rivets | Flat head rivets |
|---|---|---|
| Material is fixed together by forming a dome or snap head created by the dimple in the Set and Snap. | Material fixed together by working the end of the rivet into a countersunk hole. Used to create a flush surface finish. | Used to join sheet metal that is too thin to be countersunk. |

## Set and Snap

This is the tool used to protect and create the snap or round head rivet. It is also used to ensure the two pieces of material are firmly pressed together, or set, before riveting.

Set and snap usually used in pairs to form rivets

Snap used to form and protect the head of a snap or roundhead rivet.

**Top Tip**
Avoid the problem of alignment by drilling all the holes in one of the pieces being riveted and only one in the other. Once the first rivet has been formed drill the other holes.

Set used to ensure that surfaces to be riveted are firmly set together before forming the rivet.

| Creating a snap head rivet | Creating a countersunk rivet |
|---|---|
| (a) Drill hole for rivet and remove burrs. | (a) Drill hole for rivet and countersink. |
| (b) Cut rivet to length using end cutters. Leave 1.5 times the rivet's diameter standing for snap. | (b) Cut rivet to length using end cutters. |
| (c) Use Set and Snap to set the material. | (c) Use Set and Snap to set the material. |
| (d) Form end of rivet into a dome with ball pein hammer. | (d) Form end of rivet into a dome with ball pein hammer. |
| (e) Use snap to create the snap head. | (e) Work rivet into countersunk hole. |
| | (f) File off excess material. |

## Pop rivets

This is a method of joining thin sheet material together. The material is drilled to the correct size for the pop rivet being used. The rivet is formed using pop riveting pliers by pulling a mandrel through the rivet causing the back to swell. Once the rivet is formed the mandrel breaks off inside the rivet, tearing the head.

# Nuts, bolts and machine screws

These are all mechanical methods of joining material together. Each comes in a range of materials, diameters, lengths and head shapes.

| Nuts and bolts | Machine screws | Self tapping screws |
|---|---|---|
| Nuts and bolts come in a range of sizes with either a square or hexagonal head. They are tightened using a spanner of a suitable size and shape. Some specialised nuts have been produced, such as the wing nut, which does not need a spanner, and the locknut, which does not loosen easily. | These come in a range of lengths, diameters and head shapes and can be tightened using a screwdriver. Common shaped heads are countersunk and round heads. Machine screws are threaded to the underside of the head. | These are made from hardened steel which allows them to cut their own thread. Suitable for thin sheet metal, they are available with Philips, Pozidriv or slot heads. |

Washers are often used with nuts, bolts and screws to protect the material or to spread the load when tightened. Spring washers are used to lock the nut in position.

## Quick Test

1. State the advantage a countersink rivet has over a snap or flat head rivet.
2. State where the set and snap tool should be held when creating a rivet.
3. State which hammer would be used to form the head of a snap head rivet.
4. List three objects that have been made using pop rivets.

**Answers: 1.** It provides a completely flush surface. **2.** Set and snap set should be held securely in an engineer's vice. **3.** Ball pein hammer. **4.** Aeroplane wings, bus body panels and any other examples of pop rivets used to construct items such as kitchen utensils, furniture, etc.

# Bending acrylic

## Two methods

There are two methods used to bend acrylic in the school workshop: the strip heater and the oven. The method chosen will depend on the shape required. Both work by heating the acrylic to the correct temperature. The strip heater heats a small area and is used to create simple angled bends, freely or through the use of a former. The oven heats the entire piece of acrylic and can be used to create more complex forms using a former.

## Strip heater

The strip heater has a heating element surrounded by a reflector. This reflector focuses the heat on the small area which is to be bent. The temperature can be adjusted according to the thickness of the material. The two rails support the plastic at a safe distance from the heating element and can be set to heat different widths. Do not overheat the plastic; heat both sides to achieve an even temperature without burning the surface.

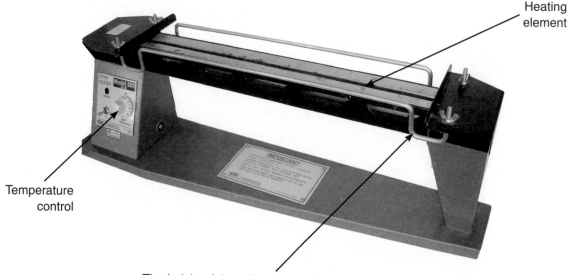

Heating element

Temperature control

The height of the rails can be adjusted to create a larger heated area.

The acrylic should be shaped and finished before it is bent, and the protective covering must be removed. Bends can be marked using a fibre tip pen or soft pencil. Accurate angles can be achieved using a wooden former.

# Oven

The oven slowly heats an acrylic sheet. The sheet will be completely flexible when heated to the correct temperature.

- 3 mm acrylic must be heated for twenty minutes at a temperature of 160–170°C.
- 6 mm acrylic must be heated for thirty minutes at a temperature of 160–170°C.

The shape is achieved by using a wooden former. Care should be taken when pressing the former together so as not to damage the surface of the acrylic.

Heating acrylic in an oven

**Top Tip**
Remember acrylic has a plastic memory – it will return to its original shape if it is reheated. So if the correct angle or shape is not achieved first time simply reheat it and start again.

## Quick Test

1. Why should the protective cover be removed from the acrylic before using the strip heater?

2. Describe why a strip heater is suitable for creating angled bends in acrylic.

3. Describe why the oven is suited to creating more complex forms in acrylic.

**Answers: 1.** It will melt and stick to the acrylic. **2.** It only heats up a narrow strip of acrylic. This limits the amount of deformation, allowing more control. **3.** The oven heats the entire piece of acrylic. This allows the acrylic formed and bent in any direction.

# Vacuum forming

## Complex shapes

Vacuum forming is used to form thermoplastic sheets into complex shapes. A vacuum former draws a softened plastic sheet to the surface of a pattern by creating a vacuum. Disposable cups, fridge interiors and packaging are some of the many products made using this process.

## Making a pattern

Before a shape can be vacuum formed, a pattern has to be made using wood, plaster or metal. The type of material used will depend on the shape required. The design of the pattern must be carefully considered to ensure that:

- the plastic sheet will fit tightly around it when the vacuum is created
- the material will not be over-stretched
- the pattern will be easy to remove from the plastic.

To ensure a tight fit, holes are sometimes drilled into the pattern, especially when creating internal corners. Tapered sides and rounded corners are also used to make the pattern less likely to stick.

A vacuum forming machine is used to heat the plastic to the correct temperature and produce a vacuum.

## Using the vaccum former

There are a number of stages required to heat and form the plastic.

- Using the lever, lower the platen and place the pattern into the vacuum box.
- Clamp the thermoplastic sheet to the frame with the toggle clamps.
- Place the heater over the plastic, heat until the plastic becomes soft and begins to sag.
- Set the controls to blow air into the vacuum box, creating space for the pattern to be raised into.
- Raise and lock the platen into place.
- Set the controls to create the vacuum to form the shape.
- Allow the plastic to cool and remove the pattern.

**Top Tip**
Reversing the vacuum, to gently blow air, as the plastic cools makes it less likely to stick to the pattern. This will ensure that the pattern can be removed without distorting or damaging the plastic shape.

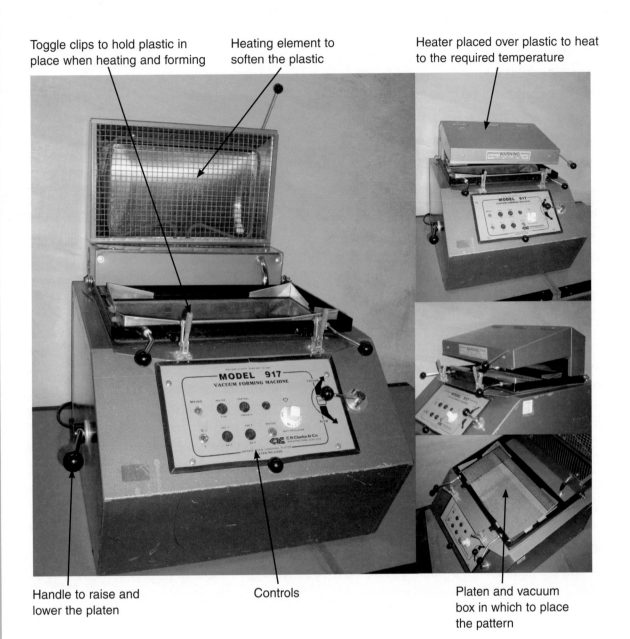

Toggle clips to hold plastic in place when heating and forming

Heating element to soften the plastic

Heater placed over plastic to heat to the required temperature

Handle to raise and lower the platen

Controls

Platen and vacuum box in which to place the pattern

## Quick Test

1. Name a suitable plastic to use in the vacuum former.

2. Describe the advantages that vacuum forming offers when manufacturing a batch of identical objects.

**Answers: 1.** Acrylic sheet. **2.** The shape only has to be created once by making a former so any number of identical products can be created quickly, efficiently and accurately.

# Finishing

Various finishes are available for use in the school workshop. The choice, application and preparation depend on:

- the material used
- the purpose of the finish
- where the product will be used
- who will use the product
- how long the product is expected to last.

Finishes can be classified under the headings of wood, metal and plastic.

## Wood

Both natural timber and man-made boards require some form of finish. A finishes can be applied to improve the look of some cheaper timbers and man-made boards or to enhance the more decorative timbers. Finishes can also be used to provide a protective layer making a project more durable, safer and weather resistant.

### Preparation

It is important to prepare the surface of the wood before any finish can be applied. In general, wood is sanded to provide a smooth surface using different grades of **glass paper**. Glass paper is available in different grades; coarse, medium and fine. It is usual to work through each grade to achieve the best finish, remembering to sand with the grain and where possible use a **sanding block**. If the project has been assembled using nails ensure that all nail heads have been punched under the surface using a nail punch. Filler can also be used to improve the surfaces prior to finishing.

**Top Tip**
Dampen the surface of wood to raise the grain before using smooth grade glass paper.

### Varnish

**Polyurethane varnish** provides a clear surface coating that enhances the natural look of the wood and provides a hard-wearing, durable surface. To achieve a good finish, two or more coats are required. Fine grade glass paper should be used to rub down the surface between coats. This provides a **key** and removes imperfections.

### Paint

Paint can provide a coloured surface coating that can be used to improve the appearance of cheaper timbers and manufactured boards. There are a wide range of different paint types: some are water-based and some are oil-based. Some paints require primers or undercoats before finishing coats can be applied. Paint can be applied using a wide range of methods depending on the type of paint, material, area to be covered or desired effect. Common methods generally used in for applying paint are:

- brush
- roller
- spray
- cloth, rag and sponge

### Stain

Stain is a method of colouring wood, it gets absorbed into the wood and requires a finish to seal and protect the surface after it has fully dried. Surfaces must be rubbed down with fine grade glass paper after stain has dried.

## Oils

Oils such as teak oil and linseed oil or olive oil can be applied to woods creating a natural finish. It can be applied with a cloth and must be allowed to dry thoroughly before recoating.

## Wax

Wax allows the natural grain structure of the wood to be seen through a satin finish. It is applied with a cloth and polished with a brush or soft cloth.

# Metals

Metals are usually finished to prevent them from corrosion or to improve the way they look. As with wood the type of finish depends on the material and purpose of the finish.

## Preparation

Steel can be finished after it has been shaped by draw filing with a smooth file. **Emery cloth** is then wrapped around a file and used with the same draw filing motion. Use coarse then fine grade emery cloth before finishing with a little oil and fine cloth. Grease can be applied to prevent the steel from rusting.

## Blueing

Blueing is an oil finish suitable for steel. After smoothing surfaces with emery cloth the steel is heated to dull red and dipped/quenched into old engine oil.

## Paint

Paint can be applied to metal with a brush or by spray painting. Once the metal has been rubbed down and degreased it will require a coat of primer followed by an undercoat and than one or two finishing coats. Wet and dry paper should be used between each coat to provide a key.

## Lacquer

Lacquer can also be applied to metal surfaces with a brush or spray paint. It provides a clear coating that prevents the surface form corrosion or tarnishing.

# Dip coating

A plastic coating thicker than lacquer or paint can be applied to a metal using a process of dip coating. This provides a durable surface that is water-resistant and insulated, and so it is suitable for use in kitchen equipment such as fridge and dishwasher shelves and racks.

Polythene powder is commonly used for dip coating. It is important to coat the metal evenly in order to achieve a good surface finish. A **fluidiser** is used to blow air through a plastic powder which allows the metal to be dipped into the plastic. This fluidisation makes the plastic powder act like a liquid and stops powder from clogging up when coming into contact with the metal.

Before an object can be dip coated it must be clean and free from grease.

The metal object is then heated in an oven to 180°C.

The object is then dipped into the fluidiser where the plastic powder fuses to the surface of the metal. This often results in the surface texture resembling an orange skin. It is then returned to the oven until the surface becomes smooth and shiny.

When dip-coating, you should take care not to overheat the plastic. You should also allow your work to cool before handling it.

**Top Tip**
Plan how and where to hold the object using wire when heating, dip coating and cooling.

# Taps and dies

## Cutting threads in metals

Taps and dies are tools that are used for cutting threads in metals. There are two types of thread that can be cut and they are known as the male (external) thread and the female (internal) thread.

## Taps

These are made from hardened and tempered cast steel and high speed steel. They are used to cut internal threads into the walls of holes that have been drilled into metal. The process of tapping a hole is described below.

- The correct size of **tapping hole** is drilled in the metal.
- A **taper tap** is used to start threading the hole.
- A **second tap** is used which deepens the thread started by the taper tap.
- A plug tap or **bottoming tap** is used to finish cutting the thread.

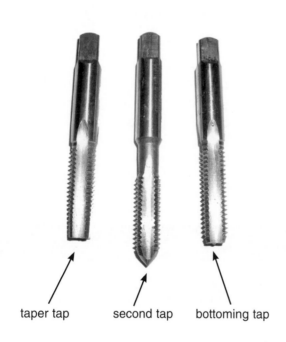

taper tap    second tap    bottoming tap

A tap wrench is used to hold the tap and provides handles to allow you to turn the tap in a forward and backward movement. The forward movement cuts the thread whilst the backward movement breaks the waste metal off, preventing the tap from clogging up.

# Dies

Split circular dies are used to cut external threads. One of these is shown in the photograph, held in a diestock holder. You will notice that there are three screws on the outside of the diestock. The middle screw lines up with the split in the circular die and all three screws can be adjusted to increase or decease the cut of the die.

The split circular die is held in a diestock holder.

- Slacken off the outside two screws, then put the die in the diestock holder, then tighten down the middle screw.

- Make sure that the bar you are threading has a chamfer on the end of it to give the die an easy start.

- Take care to ensure that the die is located and remains at 90° to the bar to avoid cutting a **drunken thread**.

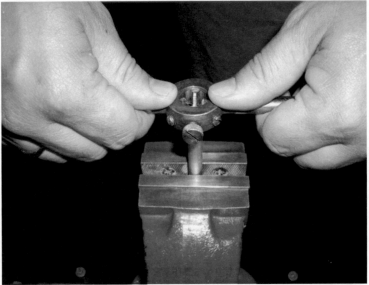

- Cut the thread using a forward and backward movement to avoid the teeth of the die clogging up.

- Check the fit of the thread by screwing it into the internal thread. If it is too tight, slacken off the middle screw and tighten the outside two screws of the diestock and repeat the whole process.

Take care to ensure that the die and the handles of the diestock are at 90° to the bar to avoid cutting a 'drunken thread'.

**Top Tip**
Use a cutting compound or lubricant on the metal to ensure that a clean and well-formed thread is made.

## Quick test

1. Explain what is meant by the term 'drunken thread'.
2. Name the three types of tap that are used when cutting an internal thread.

**Answers: 1.** This is a thread that has been cut and does not run true. It runs off at an angle. **2.** A taper tap, an intermediate tap, a plug or bottoming tap.

# Measuring and marking out

## Right tool, right job

Being able to measure and mark out accurately is vital if you are to produce quality craftwork. There are many tools available to help you, regardless of which material you are working with, and it is important that you choose the correct tool for the job.

## Metal tools

### A rule

A **rule** is used to measure lengths and is usually calibrated in millimetres. It has a zero end to allow it to measure accurately from a corner or surface.

### A scriber

A **scriber** is sometimes referred to as a metalworker's pencil. The point is made from tool steel and is used to scratch a fine line onto metal.

### Centre punches

**Centre punches** are used to mark the position of the centre of any hole to be drilled in metal. This is important to give the drill a location and stop it from wandering.

### An engineer's square

An **engineer's square** is similar to a try square but designed to be used on metal. There is a small groove cut on the stock of an engineer's square, just below the blade, to allow it to be used where a burr has been left on the metal.

### Spring dividers

**Spring dividers** can be used to draw circles and mark off arcs on metal. They are also used to step off equal lengths along a straight or curved line.

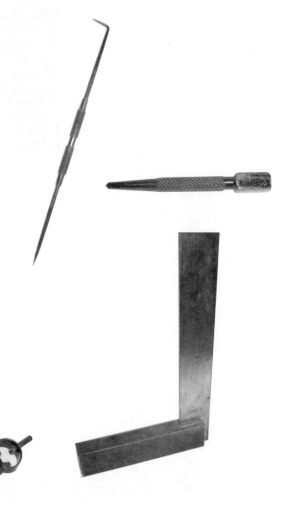

## Odd-leg callipers

**Odd-leg callipers** are sometimes referred to as 'Jenny-Callipers'. They are used to scribe a line parallel to an edge, in the same way that a marking gauge is used on wood.

## A micrometer

A **micrometer** provides a very precise and accurate way of measuring the diameter of a bar or the thickness of metal. It can measure to within 0.01 mm.

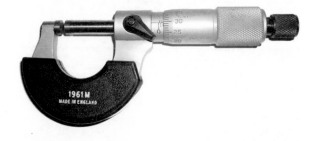

# Wood tools

## A marking gauge

A **marking gauge** is used to mark a single line parallel to the edge of a length of wood. This line is marked by a sharp metal point called a spur which can be set to a specified distance from the stock.

## A mortice gauge

A **mortice gauge** is used to mark two lines parallel to the edge of a length of wood. This gauge has two spurs which can be set apart from each other to a specified distance. It is used normally to mark out the position of a mortice.

## A try square

The most common use for a **try square** is to act as a guide to allow a pencil line to be drawn at right angles to an edge. The try square is set to an angle of 90° and can be used to test or 'try' if one surface is at right angles to another.

## Sliding bevel

A **sliding bevel** is used to mark out angles which are not at 90° to an edge. It can be set to any angle.

## Outside callipers

**Outside callipers** can be used on wood, metal or plastic to check the outside diameter of tubes, round bars or pieces of wood that have been turned. Once the callipers have been set around the material they can be checked against a rule.

## Inside callipers

**Inside callipers** are used to check the inside diameter of a hole.

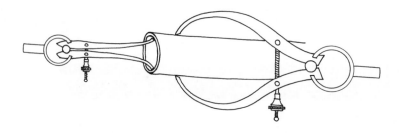

## Quick Test

1. Write down the names of two tools that could be used to find the diameter of a metal bar, other than a ruler.

2. What advantage is there to using a template when having to measure and mark out lots of identical pieces of material?

**Answers: 1.** Micrometer and vernier callipers. **2.** It saves time and is more accurate.

# Drills and bits

## Know the drill

There are several drills that you may have used or seen being used throughout your Standard Grade course. You should be able to identify the more common ones and know where they are most likely to be used.

### Twist drill

The **twist drill** can be used to drill wood, metal and plastic. The shank of the drill fits into the drill chuck and is secured with a chuck key.

### Countersink drill

A **countersink drill** is used to countersink holes in wood and metal to allow wood screws and rivet heads to sit flush with the surface of the material being drilled.

### Forstner drill

A **forstner drill** is normally used on wood to drill a flat bottomed hole.

### Auger bit

An **auger bit** is normally used with a brace to bore holes into wood.

### Flat bits

**Flat bits** are used in electric drills to drill holes in wood.

> **Top Tip**
> If the wood you are drilling starts to smoke it may be that the drill you are using is blunt. Stop the drill and ask your teacher to check it out. Large holes require a slow speed.

## Quick Test

**1.** Name the tool that would be used to drill a blind hole in 15 mm thick MDF.

**Answers: 1.** Forstner Drill.

# Files and filing

## Files for different angles and shapes

A range of files are commonly used in the school workshop. All of these work by using rows of teeth to cut or file the material into shape. Different shapes, lengths and tooth types are available depending on the shape required or material being filed. Try to choose the file that is most suited to the project.

- A **square file** can be used for small rectangular shapes.
- A **three square** is a file with an equilateral cross-section.
- **Half round files** can be used to get into tight angles and large internal curves.
- A **flat file** can be used for long, flat edges and outside curves.
- A **round file** can be used to file smaller holes or tight curves.
- **Needle files** can be used for intricate and detailed work and are available in a range of different shapes.

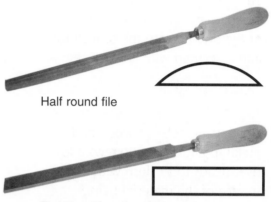

Half round file

Flat file with safe edge

A range of needle files

## Types of teeth

- **Single cut files** have one row of teeth. A single row of teeth is less likely to clog, making these files suitable for softer materials.
- **Double cut files** have two rows of teeth. A double row of teeth is more suited to medium or hard metals, and plastics.
- **Rasps** have coarse, individual teeth which remove larger amounts of material quickly and are suited to wood and other soft materials.

## Using a file

Before you file, make sure that the work is held securely, usually in a vice. Limit the amount of vibration by keeping the material being filed as close to the vice as possible. Use the full length of the file, applying just enough pressure to cut the surface in a forward motion.

# Methods of filing

There are two methods of filing used in the workshop, **cross filing** and **draw filing**.

### Cross filing

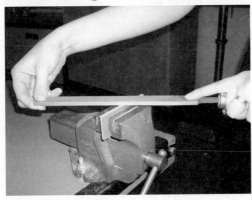

Cross filing involves pushing the file across the work at right-angles to the vice. It is effective at removing material to create different shapes and forms.

### Draw filing

This involves drawing the file sideways along the material. It is used to smooth the surface after cross filing.

Keep the file parallel to the bench when draw filing.

### File card

At times the files can become clogged as small pieces of material stick between the teeth. A file card should be used to clean the file.

# Surform

Surforms are used to create curved forms in wood or other soft materials. They are similar to files but have rougher blades and more comfortable handles. They are available in a range of shapes with blades which can be changed and replaced.

**Top Tip**
A flat file has one edge without teeth, known as a safe edge. Use this safe edge when filing internal angles to avoid filing the wrong surface.

# Planes

## Common types

Planes are very useful tools which are used to shave away thin layers of wood, allowing the workpiece to be cleaned up or reduced to the required thickness. There are many kinds of specialised planes that can be used for specific types of work, but you should know about some general types that are more common and are used often in school workshops.

### Smoothing plane

The **smoothing plane** is the most commonly used to remove any marks left on the timber and to make it flat and square. The sole of the smoothing plane is around 240 mm and it is usually 50 mm wide. You should be able to identify the **cap iron**, **lever cap** and **blade**, and be able to adjust the cut of the blade using the **lateral adjusting lever** and the **adjustment screw**.

Because the smoothing plane is smaller and lighter it is used for many types of general planing work.

### Jack plane

The **jack plane** has a longer sole than the smoothing plane at around 350 mm. It is more useful on longer surfaces and its greater length produces a flatter surface.

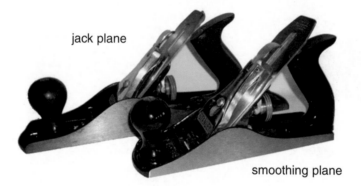

jack plane

smoothing plane

**Top Tip**
Lay the plane on its side when not in use to prevent damage to the blade.

**Top Tip**
Always check that you have set the plane properly by practicing on a spare piece of wood first. You may have to adjust the plane to remove more or less wood. Look at the shavings you have produced. Each should be the same thickness across its width. If not you may have to adjust the lateral adjusting lever to 'true up' the blade.

## Router plane

The **router plane** is sometimes referred to as a 'Granny's tooth' because of the narrow, tooth-like blade that hangs down underneath it. It is very useful for cleaning up the bottom of housings and grooves across the grain. The blade or tooth can be adjusted up or down depending on the depth required.

## Block plane

A **block plane** is used for shaping and trimming.

### Quick Test

1. Describe when a jack plane would be used in preference to a smoothing plane.
2. For what purpose is a router plane used?

**Answers: 1.** A jack plane would be used on longer lengths of wood. **2.** A router plane would be used to smooth the bottom of a housing joint.

# Hammers and mallets

## Types and uses

There are a number of hammers used in the school workshop and each one is different in size, weight and shape. Selecting the correct hammer depends on the type of work being done or the type of nails being used. Each hammer has a head and shaft held together with a wedge or taper. Holding the hammer or mallet towards the end of the shaft generates more force.

### Cross-pein hammer

A **cross-pein hammer** (warrington hammer) is a general purpose hammer. The cross-pein is used to start a nail without hitting the user's fingers. Once the nail is started, the head of the hammer can be used to drive it home with more force.

### Pin hammer

A **pin hammer** is a smaller hammer used for panel pins, tacks and small nails.

### Claw hammer

A **claw hammer** is a heavy-duty hammer that can also be used to remove nails.

### Ball-pein hammer

A **ball-pein hammer** is used for metal work. They are available in different sizes and weights. The smaller ones are usually used for centre punching and riveting. Forge work and bending require a larger, heavyweight hammer.

### Carpenter's mallet

A **carpenter's mallet** is used to hit the end of a chisel when greater force is required. The large beech head offers more control when hitting the chisel. It can also be used to assemble projects and woodwork joints.

**Top Tip**
Look at the nail, not the hammer.

## Hide mallet

A **hide mallet** is used when shaping sheet metal. The hide head of the hammer is softer than the metal and does not damage the metal's surface.

**Top Tip**
Take care not to damage and bruise the surface of the wood when driving home nails. Use a nail punch to drive the nail's head under the surface before finishing.

## Quick Test

1. What is the claw of the claw hammer used for?

2. Which hammer should be used when creating a snap head rivet?

3. Why is the head of the carpenter's mallet made from beech?

**Answers: 1.** Removing nails. **2.** Ball pein hammer. **3.** Beech is softer than metal so its use causes less damage to chisels and the work being assembled.

# Saws and sawing

## Types and uses

There are a variety of saws that you will have used in the workshop during your course. Almost every project involves cutting or sawing at some stage, so it is important that you are able to choose the correct saw for the job.

### Tenon saw

A **tenon saw** is sometimes referred to as a back saw because of the distinctive steel or brass strip which runs along its length, designed to stiffen up the thin blade. This strip prevents it from cutting through thicker material, so the tenon saw is more suited to cutting thin wood and wood joints.

A tenon saw is used for general woodwork.

### Panel saw

A **panel saw** is much longer than a tenon saw and it does not have the thicker metal strip along its length. As its name suggests, it is used to cut much larger panels such as sheets of plywood or MDF. It should not be confused with a cross cut saw or a rip saw, which are similar in appearance but are longer and have bigger teeth.

A panel saw is used to cut large boards or panels.

### Coping saw

The **coping saw** is easily recognised with its thin blade and high C-shaped frame. The teeth on the blade of a coping saw should point back towards the handle so that it cuts as the saw is pulled back. Other saws cut on the forward stroke. This saw is suited to cutting straight lines, curves and intricate shapes in thin wood or plastic. The blade can be adjusted to allow it to cut in any direction. This is done by turning the

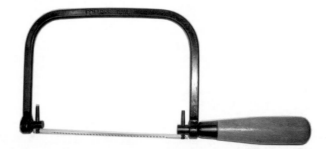

handle to release the tension on the frame and adjusting the blade by hand. Check that both pins are correctly aligned, the blade is straight and the handle is tightened before using it.

Curved cuts can be made in thinner material with a coping saw.

**Top Tip**
Saw on the waste side of the line.

## Hacksaw

A **hacksaw** is used to cut metal. It is a general purpose metalwork saw with an adjustable blade. All blades are used with the teeth pointing away from the handle, which needs to be properly tensioned before use. A variety of blades are available, and which to use depends on the type of material that is being cut. The **junior hacksaw** is a smaller version of the hacksaw, used for cutting thin metals and lighter cross sections.

Hacksaws are used to cut metal bars, tubes, plates and sheet metal.

**Top Tip**
You should use a sawing board, a bench hook or some other means of holding or clamping your wood when sawing. Be careful not to saw through onto a surface that you may damage.

## Quick Test

1. Describe how you would change a blade in a coping saw.

2. What is the purpose of the thick metal strip on the blade of a tenon saw?

**Answers: 1.** Hold the blade and frame together then slacken off the handle to release the tension in the blade. Turn the saw on its end and push down on the frame to release the blade from the pins which hold it. Insert a new blade between the pins and tension the saw by turning the handle. **2.** It stiffens the blade of the saw, making it easier to cut long straight cuts in wood.

# Vices, clamps and cramps

## Types and uses

There is a wide range of specialised tools and equipment used in the school workshop to hold, clamp or cramp material. The method used depends on the type of material and the equipment being used.

### Engineer's vice

An **engineer's vice** is used to hold metal or plastic. It is securely bolted to a bench and can be used to apply great force. It has serrated metal jaws to provide extra grip when a tight grip is needed. When working with softer metals or plastic it is necessary to use vice guards to protect the surface of the material.

### Woodworker's bench vice

A **woodworker's bench vice** is used to hold wood or plastic. It is bench-mounted with beech-faced jaws. The wooden jaws help to protect the surface of the material being cut.

### Hand vice

A **hand vice** is used to hold thin sheet material when drilling.

### Machine vice

A **machine vice** is used to hold material when being machined. It is commonly used to hold metal sections when drilling. Its jaws have been designed to hold irregular shapes and allow through holes to be drilled.

### Bench hooks

**Bench hooks** can be held in a vice or hung over the edge of a bench. They are used to hold wood while it is being cut. The bench hook prevents the wood from slipping, making the sawing action smoother and easier. Its use also stops the wood from splintering towards the end of the cut and protects the bench. It may be necessary to use more than one bench hook to support a longer length of wood.

### Bench stops

**Bench stops** form part of the woodwork bench; they can be adjusted to hold material of various lengths and thicknesses using the tail vice and stops. A bench stop is commonly used when planing long lengths of material or for cramping projects together.

# Cramps

## G-clamps

**G-clamps** are available in a range of sizes. They can be used to hold work to a bench or to cramp small projects together. When tightened, the cramp can damage the material being held so protect the surface with scrap material.

## Sash cramps

**Sash cramps** are used to cramp frames and carcases together, or when laminating. Consideration must be given to the placement and number of cramps so as to avoid the project from twisting or bowing. Care should also be taken to protect the edges using cramping blocks or scrap wood.

**Top Tip**
Remember to check for squareness or winding when cramping a project together.

## Folding bars

**Folding bars** are held in an engineer's vice to allow longer lengths of metal to be held. They are used to fold sheet metal into different shapes.

**Top Tip**
Remember to choose the correct vice for the job. Take the time to protect your work with vice guards if necessary and never over tighten the vice.

## Quick Test

1. Explain why it is important to hold thin sheets of metal in a hand vice when drilling.

2. What makes an engineer's vice more suited to holding metal when being cut, shaped or finished?

3. When creating a housing joint using a hand router, how should the material be held to the bench?

**Answers: 1.** Thin sheet material is difficult to hold firmly on the drilling table; the likelihood of it spinning is therefore higher. This would be dangerous. **2.** Serrated jaws allow the metal to be held more securely without slipping. **3.** In a woodworker's bench vice.

# Chisels

## Types and uses

Chisels are used to shape and cut wood and are particularly useful when cutting all types of wood joints. There are many different types of chisel and they are all available in a large range of sizes. Chisels are made from high carbon steel and are ground and sharpened to give a fine cutting edge. Sharp chisels are essential for quality work, but they are dangerous and should be used with care.

There are these main types of chisel with which you should be familiar.

### Firmer chisel

The **firmer chisel** has a rectangular section blade and is generally used on big heavy work where deeper joints have to be cut.

### Bevel-edged chisel

A **bevel-edged** chisel is more common and is used on most wood projects in the workshop. Its bevelled sides allow it into tight corners, which is particularly useful when cleaning up wood joints.

A bevel-edged chisel is particularly useful for cleaning out wood joints.

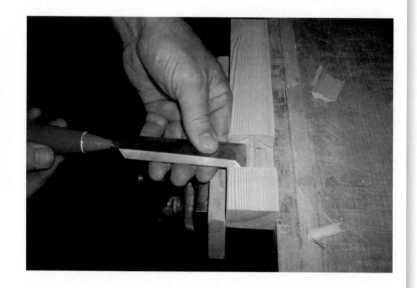

### Mortice chisel

One of the more specialised types of chisels that you may have come across is the **mortice chisel**.

As the name suggests, it is designed specifically to cut mortice joints in wood. It is a very robust chisel, able to withstand heavy blows from a mallet. It has a thick, tapered blade which allows it to lever out waste when cutting mortices, and prevents twisting in deeper mortices. Mortice chisels have a leather washer between the ferrule and the blade which acts as a shock absorber when hit by a mallet.

## Safety

Chisels are dangerous tools and they need to be handled and used with care.

- Always keep both hands behind the cutting edge of the chisel when using it.
- Never point the blade of the chisel towards your body or chisel towards your body.
- Point the cutting edge of the chisel towards the floor when carrying it.
- Put it in the well of your workbench when it is not in use. This prevents it from falling onto someone's feet.
- Wherever possible, fix or clamp your work securely when using a chisel.

**Top Tip**

When chiselling out grooves or housings be sure to turn the bevel-edged chisel over so that the flat surface faces the top. This will force the chisel up and prevent it from digging into the wood.

## Quick Test

1. What is the purpose of the leather washer on a mortice chisel?
2. Describe one safety precaution that must be observed when using a chisel.

**Answers: 1.** It absorbs the shock and vibration caused after the chisel has been hit with a mallet. **2.** Both hands should always be behind the cutting edge when using a chisel.

# Index

# Index